Not Your Usual Book!

Prepare yourself for an <u>INTERAC</u>

"The Power of I Am . . . So I Can" is jilled ...

that go far beyond the pages of this book. Find QR codes to:

- o Websites
- o Additional Books and Workbooks
- o Business Articles
- o Online Resources
- o Exercises
- o Photos
- o Audio
- o Video

HERE'S YOUR CHANCE TO START INTERACTING!

Check out this video of the authors giving you their own introduction to the book at:

https://youtu.be/9imbmxUTAzI, OR, scan the code to take you to the video!

With the Electronic Resource Hub, your available content will all dynamically change as more is learned and discovered.

Are you ready?

Keep going to learn from the powerful experiences of a driven Aussie maverick building a legacy in this interactive book that is part memoir, part business book, and all-engaging!

Testimonials

"We began working with Iain in 2008, which was a pivotal time in the motorcycle industry. His wide range of knowledge and expertise allowed us to navigate some of the most aggressive strategic, operational, and financial decisions we have made as a company, which ultimately led to our survival and position for growth. His involvement both personally and professionally has helped me secure long term financial security for my family and ensure the strength of my family of stores. Iain is a maverick and I appreciate all that he has done for me, and for us."

~Scott Fischer, Owner and CEO
SCOTT FISCHER ENTERPRISES
HARLEY-DAVIDSON DEALERSHIPS

"How to describe Iain: patient, thoughtful, humble. Always asking the right questions that others would not normally ask. Digging into details often glossed over by most. For the last seven years Iain has shared my journey growing the company to forty-eight locations in the U.S.. He introduced his IBGP business growth model to my Executive Team, which has been our foundation to our growth and success. Being from South Africa, I will never forget my quest to find a mentor in the U.S. who had the experience of big company leadership and how fortunate I was to meet up with Iain."

~Sean Campbell, Owner and CEO
THE HOME MAG

"I have known Iain for more than a decade now. He has been my business coach, my mentor, my advisor and most significantly my friend. Iain has taught me to love the business of business – from strategy to execution. We have partnered together on multiple clients around the country and I have watched this seventy-something year-old bring more energy, engagement and passion to his client service than most forty-year-olds could muster. I am so grateful that Iain took the time to write this book and share his insights and gifts with the world. Please accept the gift of Iain's mentorship with an open mind and open heart. Iain, I admire your present-future mindset and I thank you from the bottom of my heart for touching our lives!"

~Heather Christie, President
EVOLVE GLOBAL
PROFESSIONAL KEYNOTE SPEAKER
CERTIFIED EXECUTIVE LEADERSHIP
COACH

"As a martial artist, I consider Iain to be a Master Black belt in the realm of business. Iain has the rare ability to understand all aspects of business. In the martial arts, we use degrees to communicate a practitioner's rank, with the tenth degree representing mastery of body, mind, and emotions. As it applies to business, Iain is a tenth degree master in the art of business."

"Prior to working with Iain, I assumed that a business coach would have all of the "right" answers. I was educated quite swiftly, however, and soon realized that Iain would not simply give me the answers to achieve success in business and life. Instead, Iain gave me something with much more longevity and much more meaning. He asked me the right questions, at the right times, that helped me to discover the right answer on my own."

Iain enjoys the honor of performing his clients' (Jason and Angelina's) wedding ceremony.

~Jason Huett, Owner
KICK'S UNLIMITED

"Iain's insights, broad experience, and systematic approach helped us to develop systems, and more importantly, the tools we needed to measure the results. I would recommend Iain to any business that is looking to break through stagnation, develop systems and grow to new levels!"

~Tim Lightner
TWO MEN AND A TRUCK®

"Iain is a virtual CEO for hire for our business. His past experiences and dynamic leadership have helped our

company meet challenges and grow over the past twelve years from an early stage Company with two very young guys operating out of a living room to become a multi-million dollar business with our own building. Iain creates an environment for growth that can take any company to the next level."

~Steve Soliman and Colin Mehlum, Co-Owners
DIRECT NETWORKS INC

"I met Iain at ActionCOACH training in the spring of 2004. I shared his desire to help improve local businesses in our community. It has been my honor and pleasure over the last twelve years to help each other to grow our businesses, and make a real difference in our communities. I've been inspired by Iain's life stories over the years, and I'm grateful that he's written them down in this book. Thank you for sharing your wisdom my friend!"

~Jim Palzewicz, Owner
ACTIONCOACH FRANCHISE (*Milwaukee*)

"You have been so dear to (us). We are very grateful for all the time, knowledge, expertise and patience with us. Iain you are a mentor to me and a person who has helped me personally to grow and be a better business owner and mother. You are an expert at what you do and will take many more businesses to greater heights."

~Kelly Gilboy, Owner
THE WINE BOUTIQUE

"Our work with (Iain) has been the college course on business I had never had and the Business Coach (and Operational Consultant) relationship I desperately needed in order to fill the shoes of owner/manager I had grown into but never quite knew how to wear. This investment is one of the best I've made. Like solid legal or accounting counsel, working with Iain Macfarlane pays itself back ten-fold."

~Allison Gritton
GRITTON DESIGN

"Iain combines the high class of an experienced top level executive with the smile of an understanding mate. He truly listens."

~Georges Gillet-Yant
UBS

"I've spent most of my life involved with parents and siblings in a family business with varied types of retail stores and multiple sites. I engaged Iain to be my business coach five years ago at the point we were to begin a much overdue start to the succession planning for our businesses and to begin the process for me to buy the business personally. This relationship has been invaluable to me, as being based in a small town, I had few choices in finding a sounding board. Iain, without ever a hint of criticism, guides me to consider all the factors and possible results in my business and personal challenges and constantly redirects me to the issues on which I need to focus."

~Bob Lochner, Owner
ACE HARDWARE STORES (*Sauk City & Madison*)

The Power of This Book

. . . So You Can Use Your Resources

Throughout "The Power of I Am . . . So I Can," we refer to or include a number of articles on subjects ranging from goal-setting, to leadership, to conflict resolution, and more. These articles are all copyrighted to Iain Macfarlane and are reprints, sometimes with contextual editing, from original publication in the *Capital Region Business Journal* of Madison, Wisconsin. Iain was a monthly contributor to the *Capital Region Business Journal* from 2005 to 2009.

V-CAAR™ is a trademark owned by Iain Macfarlane and, when combined with other proprietary tools such as the IBGP and the Disciplined Time Management process, the V-CAAR™ becomes a tool to leave a legacy.

"The Power of I Am . . . So I Can" is a Reji Laberje Writing and Publishing interactive text. Throughout the book, you will find QR codes that will provide a little more insight into what is being shared. Some codes will take you to a website, while others will download a resource to your device.

Find a free QR scanner for your smart device via a search through your device's app store. Then, you can scan the QR codes in this book with your smart device to discover the online resources.

In addition to scanning throughout the book, much of the information from the QR codes can be found on the Electronic Resource Hub **(ERH)** for *"The Power of I Am . . . So I Can"*. Want to try it out? Visit the ERH through the QR code at the right to go to www.rejilaberje.com/iain-macfarlane.html.

"Get ready to realize

the POWER of YOU!"

~I.M.

The Power of I Am...
So I Can

How to Use Your Life Experiences to Drive Your Life's Legacy

By Iain Macfarlane

with Reji Laberje

ISBN-10: 1945907053
ISBN-13: 978-1945907050

Library of Congress Control Number: 2016914464
Reji Laberje Writing and Publishing, Waukesha, WI

CATEGORIES:
Business & Money/Management & Leadership/Systems & Planning
Biographies & Memoirs/Ethnic & National/Australian
Business & Money/Biography & History/Economic History

BISAC Codes:
BIO002000 Biography & Autobiography/Cultural Heritage
BUS043030 Business & Economics/International/Marketing
SEL027000 Self-Help/Personal Growth/Success

www.rejilaberje.com

Quantity order requests can be emailed to: publishing@rejilaberje.com

Or mailed to:

Reji Laberje Writing And Publishing
Publishing Orders
234 W. Broadway Street
Waukesha, WI 53186

Macfarlane, Iain
The Power of I Am . . . So I Can
Contributing Author: Reji Laberje
Contributing Editor: RaeAnne Marie Scargall
Interior Design: Reji Laberje
Cover Design: Michael Nicloy
Photos: Iain Macfarlane, Kimberly Laberge *(Author Photos and Iain's Home)*
Maps: Iain Macfarlane and Kimberly Laberge
Graphics: Reji Laberje

"The thing about legacies is that they don't just happen by accident."

~I.M.

The Power of Driving Your Own Legacy

. . . So You Can Choose Your Own Tombstone

"Did you do your best? What would you do differently to do better next time?"

~ Iain's Parents

*F*rom the time I was a child, my parents asked me to think about how I could improve . . . and improve . . . and continuing improvement. It became ingrained in me to evaluate myself and work toward my personal best, regardless of whether it was in the area of academics, sport, business, relationships, or anything else in life.

Their voices still ring in my ears as I hear them ask, *"Did you do your best?'* and the inevitable follow-up question: *'What would you do differently to do better next time?'*

It is my hope that, until my last day, I am learning, growing, and improving, while influencing, inspiring, and helping others to do the same. It's the legacy my parents left for me and it's the legacy that I hope to leave for those whom I've touched in my life, both personally and professionally. When I think about the legacy I'm working toward, I imagine the tombstone that is left in my place after I've gone and I strive toward the words by which I'd like be remembered.

I want my tombstone to have The Power of "I."

Iain Macfarlane

He helped others get results they otherwise would not have achieved without his Involvement, Influence, and Inspiration.

The thing about legacies is that they don't just happen by accident. The remaining memories and lessons we create occur as a *result* of the lives we've lived, the character we've demonstrated, the accomplishments we've achieved, and the relationships we've made and kept with the people we've touched.

"There is power in I *by growing away from just* I *and toward what* I *can do to make the world better. That's greater than The Power of* I*; that's*

The Power of I Am . . . So I Can."

~I.M.

"For my partner, Madge, on this adventure we call life."

~I.M.

Dedication

For fifty years, I've been working toward the legacy I chose, but I haven't done so alone. "The Power of I Am . . . So I Can" is purposefully coming out in 2016 to honor the woman who has been my partner on this adventure we call life.

For Madge; Happy FIFTIETH Wedding Anniversary!

Thank you for fifty years of children, travels, art, homes, education, laughter, businesses, books, almost-too-crazy-to-believe stories and friendships, love, successes, adventures, and a greater "power" than I ever could have achieved without you by my side.

I look forward to the many years we have left.

Table of Contents

"Never stop learning.

Never stop growing.

Never stop achieving."

~I.M.

The Power of I Am...

So I Can

How to Use Your Life Experiences

To Drive Your Life's Legacy

Iain Macfarlane, Age Four:
A shepherd to his great uncle's prized flock of
Merino sheep in Piawaning, Western Australia

Part 1
An Introduction
to Power

"I can look back today and I realize that herding my great uncle's sheep was my very first business lesson."

~I.M.

The Power of Childhood

... So You Can Reflect With Learning

"Your memories from your early childhood seem to have such purchase on your emotions."

~Dana Spiotta, American Author

I was four years old, young Alastair Iain Robert Macfarlane, known simply as "Iain" after being born in 1940. At the time, with my father still serving in the Royal Australian Air Force (RAAF) in World War II as the Commanding Officer of the Geraldton Air Base, my mother and I were living with her uncle, my great uncle, on his expansive wheat and sheep station in Piawaning, in the Outback Western Australia. My uncle had a paddock near the house where he kept fifty prized Merino sheep. These animals were valuable breeders. There were a couple of prize-breeding rams, as well. This incredible lot of valuable animals had to be let out into open fields at sunrise every day and back into the protective paddock by sunset. This job mattered because

Australia's Outback was spotted with predators, particularly dingoes.

Dingoes don't look much different than a pet dog.

Dingoes aren't quite wolves or dogs. They are now classified as a distinctive species of wild dog and they arrived in Australia three to five thousand years ago from South Asia, probably by regional sea. The often reddish-colored carnivores roamed the sweeping, wide open spaces of Australia and they would take the defenseless sheep if they were left out . . . a nice meal for a pack.

People might have stolen the sheep, as well, to keep for their breeding, wool, meat, or (more likely) to sell for a profit.

I had the job of getting up at sunrise, unlatching the big paddock gate and letting my great uncle's sheep out of the overnight protective paddock. That wasn't too difficult, but I also had the job of getting them back in at night . . . again, at age FOUR! I couldn't even see past the near pastures, much less far out beyond my field of vision where the sheep would roam each day to graze.

That's why my uncle gave me Red, a sheepdog. Red wasn't my pet; he was my colleague. I would call on Red, send him out to the places where my four-year-old eyes couldn't see the flock, and then he'd work the field, bringing in all of these special sheep. I would call Red back, wait at the gate while the animals filed in, pull the gate closed after the last one arrived, and latch it closed. (I'm sure my uncle counted the sheep, because at age four, I'm not sure I was really as accurate as I needed to be!)

I didn't recognize it until probably decades later, but I look back today and realize that herding my uncle's sheep was my very first business lesson. I had learned the **principle of delegation**.

ooooooooo

My DNA was woven initially during life in the World War II Australian Outback, and then in immediate post-war Sydney, Australia's largest city (both then and now). I was on the farm from 1941-1944 for safety due to the threat of attack from the Axis powers, sometimes by Germany and sometimes by Japan. In fact, just off the Western Australia coast, close to Geraldton, on November 19, 1941, a battle between a Leander Class Light Cruiser of the Royal Australian Navy, named the HMAS Sydney, and the German Cruiser, Kormoran, resulted in both ships being sunk. My father was the Commanding Officer of the air search. In the largest loss of life in the history of the Royal Australian Navy, the HMAS Sydney had no survivors out of its 645 sailors aboard.

After what the rest of the world saw as the end of the war to end all wars, there was still the demobilization efforts required in Australia's military. Though my father was a trained accountant, he volunteered to stay on with the Air Force for an extra year, working to help make Australia feel like Australia once again. This required my father, mother, me, and my brand new brother, Alan, to move to Sydney in 1945 as a base for my father in his demobilization service.

When living on my uncle's farm, I never felt as though I was missing out on life in a bigger city or on a bigger adventure. There were a lot of experiences and self-learning. My friends were the occasional Aboriginal children who would wander by. I didn't realize as a child how rare it was to socialize with Aborigines. Once again, it took looking back as an adult to recognize the lessons of childhood. The "New England" underway in Australia had been designed almost purposefully to segregate the "backward," as they were assumed in that era, Aboriginal children from the clean, white people . . . and mixed race children were at that time thought an outright abomination. As a child, though, a friend was somebody who treated me as a friend. **Nonjudgment became a part of me.**

ooooooooo

I was five by the time the war really ended for us. We moved from my great uncle's sheep station across the continent to Sydney on the East Coast to the home of a distant cousin of my mother.

In the home of my mother's cousin, there were two brothers, eight years and five years older than I, respectively. They were already sports focused and I followed them around everywhere. It was a well-to-do area of Sydney. I would go with the brothers, watch the older one play, and **learned to**

love competition . . . for the rest of my life. Fifteen years later, the older boy had gone on to become a competitive cricket player and we had the chance to play for different teams against each other.

Later, in 1946, when my father returned permanently from his military duties, my family was too large a group to stay on with my mother's cousin. We were nomadic like the Aborigines from my earliest boyhood.

ooooooooo

The next home we moved into in early 1946, when my father was still away in the RAAF, my mother, Alan and I moved into the house of my grandmother's two unmarried distant relatives in another suburb of Sydney, Pymble. The two older women were currently on a trip to England and they allowed us to stay in their turn-of-the-twentieth century home. While I try to reflect on that home, I don't remember much other than my mother being the one who drove me to a nearby grade school, Gordon Public School. I do recall the vacant adjoining lot belonging to the sisters, as it was dotted with persimmon and orange trees. I remember picking and eating the fruit, and then returning home sticky-faced.

The next home in Gordon was another distant relative of my Grandmother. I remember her as a very elegant person. Her home had a tennis court, a ballroom, many bedrooms and more than sufficient space for our family. I was able to walk the half mile to and from Gordon Public School where I had started earlier that year and it felt like I now had some routine and ease in my life.

I turned six in that home. I was old enough to understand that my country had been attacked. The Japanese had flattened Darwin and sunk ships in Sydney Harbour. We had been in a war and war was a very serious and scary thing. I had my own bedroom at the very front of the large house and air conditioning was nonexistent in those days, so my window was left open. At night, shadows from outside played on the curtains and, when the breezes blew, the drapery would flutter into the large, open windows. I remember lying in my bed, paralyzed with fear as I imagined the shadows being invading soldiers that could easily enter through my bedroom window.

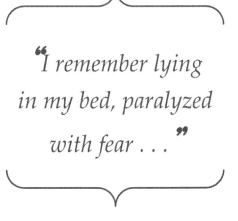

"I remember lying in my bed, paralyzed with fear . . ."

The **lessons of recognized fears and unrecognized biases** wouldn't come until years later when I bonded with a Japanese man at the East-West Center . . . but that's a story for later.

ooooooooo

A couple of months later, my father returned permanently from his military duties and my sister was due to be born shortly thereafter. We were now about to become a group too large to stay in the Gordon home. We were becoming nomadic like the Aborigines from my earliest childhood.

ooooooo

In the difficult, immediate post-war years in Australia, my father, following his military service, was unable to get work in his trained profession as an accountant. He taught himself to do upholstery as he had bought a small used furniture store in Pennant Hills (then an outer north-western suburb of Sydney). This town became my home through the remainder of grade school and high school.

Dad's work was long hours, but not much money. Then, Anne was born; we needed to move again. This time we rented a house on Hawkesbury River, forty-five miles north of Sydney. So as not to lose almost a half year of schooling, it was decided I should finish my grade one schooling in the town we were moving away from, Gordon.

Each morning, I would get on a boat with my Dad at 7:00 A.M., take it to the town of Brooklyn to catch a steam train which we hopped on for half an hour before getting onto the electric trains at Hornsby where he would go one way to his new store in Pennant Hills and I went the other way to grade School in Gordon.

"We would return home each day by electric train, steam train, and by boat."

At the end of the school day, I took two electric trains to Pennant Hills to meet up with my father while he was still working in the furniture store. At the end of his day we would return by electric train, steam train and by boat to end up home on the Hawkesbury River at 8:00 P.M.

At six-years old, I learned the importance of keeping a schedule and personal responsibility.

ooooooooo

When my grade one school year was finished, after years of living with various family members and in temporary homes, my parents bought three acres of land in Pennant Hills which was reached by an unpaved dirt road that dead ended in the bush. Little by little, over three years, the land where that Caravan parked was cleared. To be able to live on this land, Mum and Dad had a custom-made, sixteen-foot by eight-foot Caravan that the (now) five of us (me, my brother, my sister, and my parents) lived in, supplemented with a tent. Little by little over three years, the land where the caravan parked was cleared.

While our 1,200 square foot home was being built over a two plus year period—finally completed in 1949—we managed in that trailer and tent. When a garage was finished for the house, we actually took our meals and "spread out" in the garage, rather than the tent and we continued to sleep in the caravan. For what was basic living we had running water and electricity connected to the caravan, but we used an outhouse until the house was completed.

From Left to Right Alastair, Anne (2), Alan (4), Iain (8), and Margaret Macfarlane in 1948.

My parents took charge (with a little help from me) of clearing land, collecting eggs from our chickens, milking our goats, cultivating the land, growing vegetables and planting fruit trees. I came from that land. When I go back to the "little" home for visits from the States, I wonder how we survived, but we were truthfully happy.

The war was over and we were together. We were never at each other in arguments. We did what we had to do to survive . . . work hard, complete our tasks responsibly, and have honesty and integrity with one another, ourselves, and others.

" *The war was over and we were together.* **"**

Iain's Dad mans the rototiller with Iain (back left), Anne (front left), and Alan (right).

My mum had been a teacher who had gone to Sydney University (a rare accomplishment in the 1920s, particularly for women) and she was continually teaching us about:

o   Hard Work

o   Education

o   Accountability

Mostly, she taught us by proxy of her own example that there were paths to simple contentment and that your family environment could ground you and set your happiness. Mum built a foundation for us so that before my formal education had really begun and, while I was a young child, I'd already been schooled in ways that it would take a lifetime to truly recognize.

The lessons of my boyhood homes were many, from the principle of delegation learned as a four-year-old shepherd, to a six-year-old commuter, to a child with responsibilities to care for animals, plants, vegetables, and even to some of the harsh reality of surviving nature with Australia's highly venomous snakes (seven out of the world's most dangerous snakes live in Australia), and spiders, as well as from sharks when scuba diving!

Iain keeps this oil painting on masonite by Yann Pahl because it depicts the Australian desert landscape and makes him think of home. It hangs over his mantle at his home in the U.S.

A Koala Hanging Out

I'll never forget the grunting of koalas at nighttime and—at sunrise—the harsh "laughter" of kookaburras on the property where we grew up which was then on the outskirts of Sydney and on the edge of "the bush".

The "laughing" kookaburra

So You Can Reflect With Learning, ask yourself:

1 –Are there experiences from my childhood that I recognize as shapers to my emotions, thoughts, words, or actions?

2 – What people from my childhood had the greatest effect on my thoughts words, or actions?

3 – What places from my childhood had the greatest effect on my thoughts, words, or actions?

4 – What fears do I remember from my childhood?

5 – If I could choose just three life lessons reflected in my childhood experiences, what would they be?

Iain Macfarlane Today

The Power of Life Principles

. . . So You Can Know Your Coach

"We are all visitors to this time, this place. We are just passing through. Our purpose here is to observe, to learn, to grow, to love . . . and then we return home."

~Australian Aboriginal Proverb

I've spent my thirteen-year business coaching career with ActionCOACH, the leading business coaching organization in the world, operating in sixty-five countries with more than 1,000 coaches. In that role, I've thoroughly defined the vision I desire to bring forth through my coaching practice, (as well as through this book):

"I am a certified Business Coach, providing business help, business advice, business coaching and mentoring services to small and medium sized businesses.

I have a passion for helping businesses like yours grow and become profitable, so you, the business owner, can enjoy the lifestyle you choose and deserve.

As your Business Coach and advisor, I will help you deliver the results you desire using proven tools, methodologies and systems, tested and perfected over tens of thousands of businesses worldwide for more than two decades. I will hold you accountable for your results and just like a sports coach, push you to perform at optimal levels."

You can visit my coaching site online at: *http://www.actioncoach.com/iainmacfarlane*, or by simply scanning the code.

In order to thoroughly define my business coaching vision, I looked back at the decades of experiences that preceded its commencement and consciously identified the principles in place in my life and which might be valuable to others. These tools became my seven life principles.

ooooooooo

There is a story that has made its way around the internet and social media about how one is affected by the world around him or her and how, in turn, one affects his or her world. The story's origins are attributed to everyone from Nancy Reagan to anonymous brides to early British royals, but the lesson remains the same:

A young woman went to her mother and told her about her life and how things were so hard for her. She did not know how she was going to make it and wanted to give up. She was tired of fighting and struggling. It seemed that, as one problem was solved a new one arose.

Her mother took her to the kitchen. She filled three pots with water. In the first, she placed carrots, in the second she placed eggs, and the last she placed a tea bag.

Her mother turned the three pots on high, and then let the pots sit and boil, without saying a word. In about ten minutes, she turned off the burners. She fished the carrots out and placed them in a bowl. She pulled the eggs out and placed them in a bowl. Then, she ladled the tea into a bowl.

Turning to her daughter, she asked, "Tell me what you see?"

"Carrots, eggs, and tea," she replied.

The woman brought her daughter closer and asked her to feel the carrots. She did and noted that they were soft. The woman then asked her daughter to take an egg and break it. After pulling off the shell, she observed the hard-boiled egg. Finally, the mother asked her daughter to sip the tea. The daughter smiled, as she tasted the bittersweet, fragrant blend.

The daughter then asked, "What's the point, mother?"

*Her mother explained that each of these objects had faced the same thing—boiling water—but each had reacted differently. The carrot went in strong, hard, and unrelenting. However, after being subjected to the boiling water, it softened and became weak. The egg had been fragile; its thin outer shell had protected its liquid interior. After being through the boiling water, though, its insides became hardened. The tea leaves were unique, however. After they were in the boiling water, it was the **water** that had changed.*

"Which are you?" she asked the daughter. "When life is occurring around you, how do you respond? Are you a carrot, an egg, or tea leaves?"

The experiences we have fill our tea bags; they are the leaves of lessons. Our memories are literally the spice of life; our accomplishments, the fruits of our labors; our relationships, the overtones. If you take the time to fill your tea bag, it creates a blend that is uniquely you and it's up to you to change the world around you with it.

The lessons, accomplishments, experiences, memories, and relationships I had in my early days created the means to accomplish my legacy. Learning from life provided me with personal drivers and life principles that I knew could have a positive effect on the world, if I allowed them to do so.

oooooooo

1. <u>Honesty, Integrity, and Sincerity</u>

This driver comes from my parents and their parents before them.

1. Always tell the truth.

2. Do what you say you'll do.

"It's important to live principled lives, even if it means sacrifice."

These two steps to honesty, integrity, and sincerity are more important than anything else. Sometimes you have to make tough decisions, even the decisions that you feel in your heart are right. Those stories, and the decisions made in them, make us who we are . . . our lives are biopics. It's important to live principled lives, even if it means sacrifice. *Living with honesty, integrity, and sincerity is a matter of being able to stand by the tough things and not give in.*

2. <u>Continuous Learning and Growth</u>

Without a doubt, the driver of learning comes from my mother. She was the first member on her side of the family to go to university. In the 1920s at the time she went to the University of Sydney, only five percent of attendees were women. Her parents made sure that all of their kids had a great education, but Mum was the oldest. She was always intellectual; she always

> *"She encouraged me to always search for something new that I did not know about before."*

was inquisitive, wanting to know about things. That desire transferred to me. Mum would ask me to talk about things, but I had to have the knowledge to talk about them with her. She encouraged me to always search for something new that I did not know about before.

The classic "Biggles" stories can still be found.

I read stories from the time I was very young, and it was Mum who taught me to read. I remember that, after lights out, I would read with a flashlight under the covers. My favorite stories were Ion Idriess young adult books about life in the Outback Australia and stories about the aborigines. I also read *Biggles*, a fictional English Royal Air Force hero from World War II and fancied myself as a writer that took my own stab at creating stories! Stay tuned to the Electronic Resource Hub; soon you'll be able to find my early story, *Out of the Blue*. (Scan the code!)

When I went to University, I always wanted to go beyond the required reading, and know more about what we were studying. I always had a thirst to grow more and I needed to grow my own breadth of knowledge. *That drive for more knowledge has paved the way for much of my work throughout life.*

3. <u>Physical Development and Health</u>

My parents were always healthy. We always ate nutritious food; when we were building our home and for a number of years after that, we grew and raised our own food; vegetables and fruits, chickens for eggs and meat, and goats for milk. Maybe it was the experience my mother had when the nearest store—when we lived at her Uncle Arthur's farm—was an hour away.

In addition, my parents were both athletic. My father was a very good athlete who could have done more in the sporting world as an international rugby player for Scotland, or as a professional soccer player for Aberdeen. Instead, his early career as a Managing Agent for wealthy absentee property owners in the Far-East took him to Malaya, Borneo and Burma (he did play for the Burma soccer team). And, in 1939, he became a part of World War II in the Royal Australian Air Force (RAAF). At that time, his military services stopped his pursuits of an athletic career. My Mum always participated in athletics, as well, and supported us in our sporting endeavors. She continued to play tennis until she was eighty-four.

I played every sport I could in grade school and high school including cricket, rugby, tennis, golf, track, table tennis and field hockey and—for the next four years—I represented the University of Sydney in three sports; cricket, squash, and baseball. The whole, natural foods that my mother prepared, the sport and work activities we experienced in our daily lives, and the fact that we didn't have alcohol as a regular addition to meals led to good health. I never ever smoked or did drugs because I wanted to be good in sports. Athletic involvement gave me enough *discipline* to stay healthy, because I wanted to be the best. I didn't want to run the risk of damaging my opportunities to be good. My brother was a top level middle and long distance runner, too, and we consistently associated with others who were athletically successful. One of our good friends became Captain of the Australian Commonwealth Games Team. In cricket, one of my buddies made the Australian Team; I also had friends who played for the Australian Rugby Team. We were surrounded by international-level athletes.

I learned to enjoy feeling good and healthy.

I encourage people to know that the physical part of life is important in order to perform at your best. I started playing competitive sports when I was about ten and it became an important part of my life ever since with most of my focus and passion today being for golf, a sport in which I am still competitive at my current age.

4. Spiritual Beliefs

I was christened Presbyterian. However, when we settled into our home in Pennant Hills, there was no Presbyterian church, so we went to church at a Church of England (Episcopalian) church. My parents weren't dogmatic.

I had my own bible and my parents were good believers, but not evangelistic or charismatic. In my growing up years, Australia was almost equally Protestant and Catholic and certainly over ninety percent Christian. We weren't exposed to other religious influences.

The way my parents used religion was to instill principles. When I went to my private high school, Barker College, it was Church of England, relatively laid back, and low key. We had chapel service every day, so it was part of my involvement in school. It was the principles taught that became an element of my life more than the doctrine. Much like these seven principles I'm sharing, spirituality became a guide to living well and right.

In my final high school year, I played a significant role as a student in school life and I was a Prefect. We were responsible for a significant amount of the routine daily discipline in the school. We even had to dole out punishment. It was a tremendous responsibility. Occasionally—in this role of prefect—I had to read the lesson of the day in chapel. It forced me to reflect on the teaching.

At University, I had very little formal religion, but at the East-West Center where I next attended, I took comparative religions and worked side-by-side with others who had different beliefs. It was my first real exposure to other viewpoints and, through that experience, I became more spiritual than religious.

I knew that it was important to respect other religions as they also serve to provide spiritual guidance to their followers. I recognize that there is something more powerful than I am and, by respecting that, it also allows me to also respect other people and who they are based on their value systems. *Spirituality feeds respect.*

5. <u>Respect and Trust</u>

When I meet with people in any environment or setting, I make a conscious effort to start with an attitude of respect and trust. Their life principles to that point might not be the same as mine. Odds were that we had different fitness and nutrition ideals, different educational backgrounds, different spiritual backgrounds, and certainly different cultural and national identities. I also, at least subconsciously, look for a comparable reflection of respect and trust back to me and who I am as a person. If I become aware that another person is violating that relationship, I will do my best to discuss my thought on the situation. However, with limited time and energy in my life, I need to know when it's okay to walk away.

 Because confrontational discussions can be difficult, at best, consider reading this resource on the subject found at https://goo.gl/ffAarw titled, *Failure to Deal with Confrontation – It's An Excuse. (Use the QR code at left.)*

> **"There's that fine line I had to walk to ensure I stayed confident without becoming egotistical."**

During the period of time in which I was a Fellow at the East-West Center from 1962-1964, there was a time when I may have modeled a level of arrogance because of the amount of success that I'd already achieved in life. I was never aggressive about it, and there's that fine line that I had to walk to ensure I stayed confident without becoming egotistical. I needed to come to understand that others doing things differently could be as good as I was.

Though I had success in my approaches, those were not the only principles to achieve success.

6. <u>Ambition and Attitude</u>

I recognized in my parentage that both of my parents had been incredibly successful and always were high achievers, but it was in a very low-key way. Their accomplishments weren't pushed on people. They were modestly hard-working. My father became the highest ranked officer of all of the volunteers in the RAAF in World War II. My mother was one of the very few women to break through and get a University degree. On my mother's side, those whom I knew well in Australia, I had both uncles serving with honor and glory in World War II, one in the Indian Army because that's where he

> *"I was witness to an ambition to be successful."*

was living when the war broke out. That uncle parachuted behind Japanese lines in Burma and was never caught. The other uncle flew planes in New Guinea. My two aunts, when the war broke out were visiting England and they joined the Royal Air Force as ambulance drivers in London. Nobody ever sat on the sidelines.

Within the family I knew and loved, I was witness to an ambition to be successful. The generation of my parents set for me a level of success that made me subconsciously want to do things well. I didn't know there was another option.

I competed from the youngest age and the will to win happened from those earliest years. I always wanted to be on the best, the winning team. I remember when I played on an "Under-Fourteen" district field hockey team and we won the Sydney championship. I had broken my nose with a stick to the face in the semi-final. However, I played in the final the next weekend with a broken face because I wanted to be there . . . ambition creates a positive attitude. There isn't allowance for anything else. You always keep reaching.

At Sydney University, where I attended, the motto at the time (translated from Latin) meant *"reaching for the stars"*. At my high school, Barker College, the motto was *honor non honores "honor, not honors."* But, long before then, my family gave me simply the motto of *"Do your best . . . then work to get better!"*

7. <u>Legacy and Desire</u>

When I spoke about legacy, I focused on that tombstone statement that we each define for ourselves and then work to achieve, such as:

> *He helped others get results they otherwise would not have achieved without his Involvement, Influence, and Inspiration.*

The question each of us needs to ask ourselves is: "What would I like people to say about me at my memorial? What do I want said by family? Friends? Professional connections?"

Before those words are said, considering what they might be should help to build a self-desire to achieve that legacy. One can't have true desire without a legacy plan and what that legacy is, or how it can evolve and be achieved. What is desired at "The Final Opportunity" to reinforce the legacy? The more you learn and understand, the more your legacy changes over time. Nonetheless, it's important to have the desire to identify a legacy, even with the knowledge that it may change as you have more experiences and as you get older in your career and personal path.

First – Visualize your life to create a desire to set a legacy.

Then – Allow that legacy to drive your desire to build that life.

As I have mentioned previously, my parents often said to me, in the very words that have guided my seventy-six years:

"Did you do your best?"

"What could you do differently

next time to do better?"

These two questions should chase us as we chase legacy with desire and desire with legacy.

"Do your best . . .

then work to get better."

~I.M.

Iain Macfarlane

The Power of Experience

... So You Can Get Ready

"An unexamined life is not worth living."

-Socrates, Philosopher and Writer

Robert Hughes, in his worldwide bestselling title *The Fatal Shores: The Epic of Australia's Founding*, teaches that we can learn from the pride of rebellion (and an Australian inferiority complex). I never personally felt inferior. When I became successful in the U.S., I reflected with a high level of pride on my native Australia. In my era, a century after the convict-centered founding, I knew a different country. One that was vibrant, energetic, and taking up its positive place in the world.

At the end of World War II, the population of Australia was just over seven million; by the time I got to the U.S., it had reached about ten million; and today, Australia has over twenty four million people. While twenty four million may seem like a large number, when one considers that the population of Greater Los Angeles, alone, is nearly nineteen million, perspective is gained on the relatively sparse population of Australia (Australia is an area larger than Continental U.S.).

I question whether there was an inherent feeling of inferiority that drove Australians to be better . . . to prove that we were as good as the rest of the world. Was there something in the rugged history? Or was there something in our genes? Maybe it was a bit of both.

> "*The island continent was a barren, rough and tough place . . .*"

The convict history of Australia is well-known. The island continent was a barren, rough and tough place from which it was thought nobody could escape. Once British prisoners left the British shores for Australia, they were gone forever. For eighty years from 1788 to 1868, 164,000 convicts were brought to the prison colony, as though that would just erase them from existence and stop their family trees. Nobody ever realized that their descendants would become world competitors in sports, business, medicine, science, education, and academics. The convicts had been written off.

Part of the isolated convict history of Australia built in a desire to . . . well . . . escape! As a young Australian growing up, it was an inherent cultural belief that when you completed your education, high school or college, you went overseas to see the world. Australians have always been known as the great hitchhikers of the world. The mindset was that you would take off and see the world with the anticipation of coming back to make a difference in our own country.

When I finished attending University of Sydney in December 1961, I left after Christmas and hitchhiked around New Zealand. I spent three months there from January - March, hitchhiking on the two main islands.

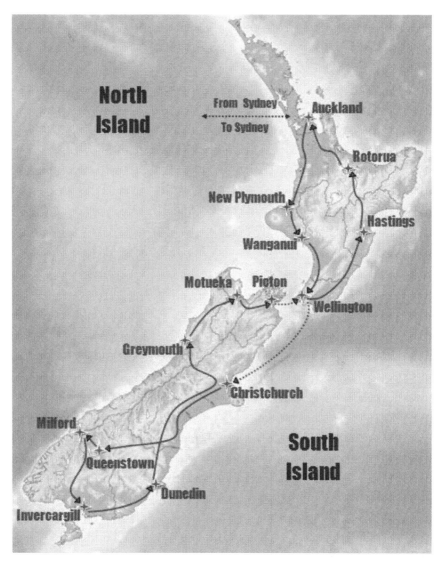

A map of Iain's New Zealand hitchhiking travels.

I traveled by ship to Auckland, by hitch hiking to Wellington, to an Inter-Island boat that took me to Christchurch on the South Island. I spent two thirds of my time on that island. I hitchhiked to Mount Cook, which is snow covered year round on its peak. I went to the large inland lake, Lake Wakatipu, where you can find the cleanest water in the world; fishermen swear that you can actually see the fish take the hook.

On a boat ride across Lake Wakatipu I met two young post-graduate Americans also hitch hiking New Zealand and the three of us took three days to hike over the mountains, on a barely worn hiking path, seeing wildlife from wild boar to deer, to plenty of wild sheep (in the early 1980s, New Zealand had twenty-two sheep to every human!). The mountainous landscape was natural and seemingly untouched and we didn't see another human on this three day trek.

New Zealand; land of beautiful landscape and the sheep that graze upon it.

After the three days, we arrived in Milford. It was early in the morning, around breakfast time. We were unshaven and dirty, so we found what was (then) a brand new hotel: The Milford Sound Resort. We went into the restroom to clean ourselves up, when another man walked in and offered to buy us breakfast. It turned out to be Sterling Moss . . . world's greatest Grand Prix driver at the time. He was relaxing before a race in Invercargill.

My encounter with Moss was one of several lifetime brushes with the life of driving and racing. The first had occurred three years earlier, when I was nineteen and living in Sydney while going to University. As a personal challenge, I entered a contest to find the best car driver in all of Sydney. It began with over 500 entries and a one hour written exam that we all took together in the main hall of the Sydney Town Hall. I came in fifth place in that part of the contest. The top 100 were then eligible to compete in the driving and skills part of the contest. The driving involved skills and maneuverability in a number of situations, as simulated on the Sydney Showgrounds. The final part of the contest was a twenty minute drive through the inner city streets of Sydney with trap-like situations set throughout the course to observe the way each driver would respond to obstacles.

Iain with his "Best Driver in Sydney" trophy, as he appeared in the 1959 paper.

People would step out in the crosswalk unexpectedly (but still safely) to measure reaction, for instance. I won and made the front page of the Sydney Morning Herald. As the contest winner, I didn't really have an answer that time for my parents as to what I could do better next time.

Three years after winning that contest, on my New Zealand trip, I continued on my hitch hiking adventure following my meeting with Moss in Milford. My own adventures included a trip to Invercargill, but not for the race!

Then, I went back to Christchurch and crossed over on the main highway from the east coast to the west coast of the southern island, from where I found rides to Motueka on the northern part of the South Island. As I'd run out of money and couldn't afford the ticket on the Inter-island ferry boat from Picton to Wellington on the North Island, I spent ten days as a migrant worker, tobacco picking. The firm provided free accommodation of barracks and food. All sorts of young people would be passing through during their summer hitchhiking and took short term jobs tobacco picking. From Motueka, I moved on to Picton, then by ferry boat to Wellington, and hitch hiked up the east coast. I then stopped in Rotorua for a fascinating experience of exploring the home of the Maori culture. Rotorua is not only the home of the Maori people, but it also is known for world-famous geysers and hot springs. From Rotorua, I went back to Auckland to take the ship home.

My post-graduate hitchhiking was a first time I had truly been on my own. It was unknown and out of my comfort zone. Everything was a great learning experience: gaining my true self-confidence, meeting others, foreign country even though English was the primary spoken language. As I got away from my homeland, I saw many of those explorative traits in more and more of my Aussie brothers. I could recognize the role that Australia played in its own disproportionate global success in so many fields of endeavor. There was inherent honor and ruggedness that came from the Irish (who were the guards of the prison colonies), the convicts, and the immigrants. The land itself provided the openness, the arid ground, the Aboriginal tribes, the beaches (and the sharks), the gamblers, the Great Barrier Reef, the wines, the beers, the hitch hikers, the wanderlust, the ruggedness, the warrior spirit, and even the cultural inferiority complex played into a results-focused, win-desiring generation of Australians.

> *" . . . the openness, the arid ground, the Aboriginal tribes, the beaches (and the sharks), the gamblers, the Great Barrier Reef, the wines, the beers, the hitch hikers, the wanderlust, the ruggedness, the warrior spirit . . . "*

In today's world, every Australian tries to find a way to show that they came from a convict background, as a matter of pride. Ironically, my father, who came from Scotland, had a convict in his family tree who had been a ring leader of the

Scottish rebellion against England in 1820, while my mother, an Australian native from the early settlement under Governor Macquarie in 1810, did not have a convict-rooted family tree.

Since I've been living in the U.S., I've been continuously reminded and somewhat amazed at the success of Australians who have taken on the challenge and found success in many fields throughout the world. My own children are dual citizens and it was only after Australia allowed dual citizenship that I shared this honor with them in September 2003.

As much as my personal history is a rich part of my success journey, so is my cultural history.

I don't share the childhood stories of my (many) first homes or my Australian homeland simply for the sake of nostalgia. In my current life as a business coach, as well as a consultant for entrepreneurs and business owners, I've learned to study the background and culture of the people with whom I work as a part of learning to guide and influence them. Well past the actual lessons of my childhood, there was the awareness necessary for recognizing the personal and individual lessons that life brings to us.

Your journey may not include rounding up sheep or commuting with your father as a very young child, but you have your own experiences that lead to your own lessons and—in those lessons—there is power.

Today, a person can pick up any number of great books that tell him or her how to improve business and personal lives from the inside to the outside and back in again. There is valuable, worthy *knowledge*, or the cognitive understanding of information freely available in our information and digital age.

Having knowledge at our fingertips hasn't necessarily made us all immediately and immensely more prosperous, though. It certainly hasn't made us create stronger legacies, either.

In order to turn The Power of lessons into a tool for prosperity, it is important to move from knowledge to *skill*, to awareness and then, critically, to application of the information gathered.

In reflection, it's easy for me to see the lessons and the knowledge that were all around me in childhood. They went beyond my nomadic early home life. I had a private school secondary education with a focus on *learning, discipline, health, sports,* and *spirituality.* At one school vacation, I had a job delivering telegrams that required *time sensitivity* and *emotional involvement.* At another time I spent a full summer vacation riding my bike eight miles each way for a ten-hour work day picking and packing oranges; this required *discipline* and *fortitude, physical* strength and *overcoming* boredom to complete a six week task I had committed to.

We had no phone in our caravan, so we needed to *build community* with those around us, family and friends. Yet, all of those lessons impacting me for all those early years didn't eject a fully successful businessman into adulthood. I was merely in the knowledge gathering stage of my life experiences, not in the skill application of it.

In addition, the knowledge itself is different for each individual. Some programs, while well-meaning, only create a single set of goals that work well for a single businessman or woman without regard for the differing histories, cultures, or legacy visions of unique individuals.

"The Power of I Am . . . So I Can" will seek to get you to look back at your own experiences to reflect on learning, a Past-Present Mindset, while at the same time setting your mind for your future success in life and your legacy by introducing you to a critical mindset:

- o PRESENT-FUTURE Mindset

Next, you will discover the Integrated Business Growth Process, or IBGP, a strategic planning, operational, management and leadership tool to lead you toward achieving *your* specific vision, goals, and business and personal success.

In order to keep you tracking toward your vision, you'll work with the V-CAAR™, an analytical tool that takes LIFE into account, allowing realignment and recognizing that even when we work toward specific goals, those objectives may need modifying, or Reforecasting, from time to time. Nothing in our lives is forever static, it is how each of us reacts to, and makes changes, that will impact our level of success.

Finally, a backwards-by-design Disciplined Time Management Tool will help tie all of the other tools together to help you gain lifetime personal and professional achievement and legacy.

What makes *"The Power of I Am . . . So I Can"* different from other leadership books is that each of the tools shared in the context of your PRESENT-FUTURE Mindset requires your own: Life experiences, Purposes, and Visions.

Your goals are likely very different from my own or from the many other entrepreneurs that make up the economic engine of our international marketplace.

A person's life, in its stories has the benefit of, not self-promoting, but discovering points of value. You can tell your life story, but those who hear it should find some benefit in it.

My ultimate goal for this book is that it could be beneficial to another person. That's part of *my* legacy. The process of creating legacy, whether personal or professional, is entirely your own and, just as I do in life, I'm here to coach you through it.

The lessons I've learned to mold that coaching come from my own life experiences.

Time Frame	Iain's Personal Experiences	Notable Events and Activities in the World
1940-1945	Early childhood — first remembered years of life spent in the Outback of Western Australia	World War II
1945-1946	Iain's "nomadic family experiences life in many homes and with many friends and family members	Post World War II
1947-1951	Living in caravan while his family built a home; the house took so long to build because there were no building materials available in a post-war economic downturn; grade school; introduction to sports through cricket and rugby	In Australia, there was a slow economic recovery with very few resources; business didn't come back as quickly as it did for Europe and the U.S.; sheep and agriculture were still the primary economy
1952-1957	Maturation through high school; academic and athletic growth	Korean War and start of Cold War; Melbourne Olympics in 1956
1958-1962	Sydney University with major in economics and accounting; represented University in cricket, baseball, and squash, in December 1961, volunteered for Vietnam, but due to cartilage removal a year earlier (after years of rugby), was rejected in physical	Space Race accelerated after the launch of Russia's Sputnik 1; Vietnam begins . . .

1962	New Zealand hitchhiking as a post-graduation tour	Expansion of the Cold War
1962-1964	East-West Center; in the summer of 1963, met Madge in Mexico; took 9,000+ miles of bus trips through the U.S. and Mexico; attended Columbia University in New York City	Cuban Missile Crisis, U.S. Civil Rights Era led by Dr. Martin Luther King, Jr., John F. Kennedy Assassination; Vietnam escalation
1964	Asia/India Trip	Awareness of social consciousness; The Beatles on Ed Sullivan for first time; additional awareness of peace corps and related humanitarian efforts
1965 – 1966	Moved to Pittsburgh with Heinz; married Madge in 1966; first exposure to the "REAL" business world	The Space Race was REALLY ON, NOW!
1967-1972	Moved to Heinz Australia in Melbourne; in 1969 and 1971, had two more sons (Rob and Jeff) to join their half-brothers, Doug and Den; two years as Lecturer at Monash University in evenings	The final escalation of Vietnam War under Johnson; landing on the moon; U.S. protests and the hippies era escalates to a social revolution; Woodstock and the start of the drug-era/culture
1972-1977	While with "SPASM" (advertising agency), represented Pizza Hut International marketing where we brainstormed what is now the "Hawaiian Pizza"; innovative marketing and retail advertising approaches to counter the economic collapse;	Collapse of world economy and, specifically, the Aussie economic collapse from 1975-1977; terrorist attack on Summer Olympic Games at Munich

1972-1977 Contd.	developed *World Series Cricket* concept with Kerry Packer to launch to the international forefront in 1977; went to Harvard Business School (1977)	
1978-1984	Moved family to New York, to the center of the advertising industry with Doyle Dane Bernbach (DDB); Polaroid advertising internationally covering thirty-two countries (1978-1980); involved in over 400,000 miles per year of international travel making several worldwide trips and averaging more annual miles than most pilots; Atari advertising launch with Pac-Man and Space Invaders (1981-1983) with travel now to the west coast in what would become Silicon Valley; Development of Ten-year business strategy for DDB	Impact of *World Series Cricket* took effect, Cold War Arms Race; extremely high interest rates worldwide; Iran hostage situation resolved
1984-1986	Recruited by venture capitalists to turn around and sell off Power.Base for desktop computers; boys were now in High School and stepsons (upon the return to the U.S.) moved right into the work force	Reagan and Gorbachev explore global cooperation with Margaret Thatcher involvement; social global issues include Apartheid, AIDS, African Hunger and Poverty; launch of Apple™

1987 – 1993	Recruited to Knoxville Tennessee as Division President of breakthrough marketing communication company (Whittle Communications) to handle Procter& Gamble custom communications including Crest toothpaste and increased market share through communications placement in dental waiting rooms throughout the U.S.; recruited by venture capitalists to work as CEO of Knox International (which bought Michigan Bulb Company); continued through the sale of the company; Father died in April of 1993	Berlin wall falls in 1989; strengthening of the Earth Day and anti-pollution movements; sons Rob and Jeff complete college (to impact the world!)
1994 – 1996	Following sale of Knox International, returned to Australia for a couple of months, as his father was dying; made arrangements with mother to place father in hospice; consulted to create a business plan for a Therapeutic Skin Care Company (Lansinoh Laboratories) with FDA approval; was requested to join company as Chairman and CEO and gained distribution in	The prosperity economy including the evolution of technology and internet; the aging hippie era and boom of plastic surgery and beauty and youth treatments

1994 – 1996 Cont'd	Wal-Mart, Walgreens, CVS, and other leading pharmacies	
1997- 1999	Recruited for a turnaround for direct mail "How To" (DIY) book publishing company in Minneapolis; improved direct mail publishing performance, then extended direct mail distribution to National magazine brand names with selected content and also launched into traditional book retailers; licensed leading consumer branded magazines (e.g. Black& Decker, Outdoor Life, Hunting & Fishing, Field & Stream,etc), with content to create do-it-yourself (DIY) books; Modified and launched unique coffee table book for leading National Geographic photographer, Jim Brandenburg, to become the best ever selling photo-journal and personal challenge book; published photo biography of Shah of Iran; Sold company to McClatchy Newspapers (The McClatchy Company Publishing Company)	Consumer Economy, Exploding technology/internet boom leading to bubble

2000-2001	Recruited by Pleasant Rowland (American Girl) to build publishing division of American Girl brand and develop a launch plan for international expansion, to be based in London; Visited mother after her strokes and before she passed in 2000	Y2K and the burst of the tech bubble
2001	After Pleasant Rolland left American Girl, I also left to work with brother in London on creating new technology (conceptualized by Alan) for banks to move money, internationally, real-time (thirteen trillion dollars per day) to save an average of three days' interest; a working model of the product was set to be demonstrated in London—with me flying in with the developer to present a demonstration model—on September 13th and 14th . . . the opportunity fell through after 9/11 . . . couldn't arrange any more meetings; saw the second tower hit over breakfast with Madge—neither of us believed our eyes and we had an overwhelming emotional fear for our son, Jeff, who was a Marine stationed at	9/11 and a changed world . . . the beginning of Global Jihadist Terrorism

2001 Cont'd	Quantico, a potential target; he was fully armed serving his duty on the otherwise evacuated base minus he and a few other Marines.	
2002 – 2003	Sought out by a bank to turn around a manufacturing company in Belprie, Ohio, commuting weekly from Madison to Headquarters in Columbus, OH; personally went to China to make sure any labor decision did not involve sweatshop workers; son Rob moved to Madison, Wisconsin for his residency at UW Hospital in anesthesiology (with his family) and I made a Christmas decision with Madge to leave the business, now in good financial shape, in order to be with family in Madison	Union Breaking and Union Protests, Terrorism, Civil Disorder, and invasion of Iraq (son Jeff in USMC spent Iraq launch in Pentagon twenty-four/seven)
2004	In 2004, son, Jeff spent almost nine months in Iraq and at the Battle of Fallujah and also in Najaf . . . you go to bed, you shut your eyes, but your brain never sleeps waiting for the call you hope doesn't come	Continuing War on Terror . . . war is a life experience without *power* . . . I hadn't felt that way since the curtains blew into my childhood bedroom window after World War II
2004 – Present	Needed to have some professional involvement, thought about consulting, but in writing out a plan,	Housing market bubble and bust; start of global economic downturn; explosion of internet for

2004 – Present Cont'd	discovered biz coaching was more aligned to my personal style of executive influence; chose ActionCOACH because it was an experiential and relational model with a vision of "World Abundance through Business Reeducation" versus project-oriented consulting; over past twelve years, became highly-recognized, award-winning business coach including election to Global Coaching Hall-of-Fame in 2012	new tools of communication; social networking creates an international borderless community

"The Process of creating legacy,
whether personal or professional,
is entirely your own and—just as
I do in life—in this book, I'm here
to coach you through it."

~I.M.

Part 2
Learning from Experiences

"A person's life, in its stories has the benefit of, not self-promoting, but discovering points of value."

~I.M.

The Power of the Drivers for Success

. . . So You Can Connect the Personal to the Professional

"The world's societies suffer from the current cult of victimization because its subtle dogma holds that circumstances and other people prevent you from achieving your goals."

-Roger Connors, Author

A person is created and motivated through principles; but one's actions occur through drivers. For me, there are five drivers which I believe lead to life success. These drivers are chosen attitudes which push a person toward his or her tombstone statement, as well as the smaller goals that happen along the way.

In short, drivers are the very tools that will take a person to achievement of life legacy. They are critical to the endeavor. Whether driven by integrity, health, spirituality, respect, ambition, or other such concepts, developed through individual experiences, one must identify those success drivers which are in alignment with, and the necessary choices for, his or her personal legacy goals.

My five drivers for success were discovered through my six decades of life experiences and, looking forward, I see myself continuing to use them for the decades I have left to build a legacy.

1. <u>The Line of Choice</u>

The *Line of Choice* was initially published in the 1994 book by Roger Connors, Tom Smith, and Craig Hickman, titled, *"The Oz Principle."* This concept consciously became a part of my everyday life when I became an Action Coach in 2004 with ActionCOACH Business Coaching where founder, Brad Sugars, is one of the most prominent proponents of the *Line of Choice* concept. However—in reality—I had been living out this concept through most of my life.

The *Line of Choice* distinguishes between a mindset of achieving **results** versus giving **reasons** for why a result has not been (or cannot be) achieved. The Line of Choice acknowledges a difference between **leaders** and **followers** in any field of life. It's not an easy principle; the concept *is* very easily understood, but not often applied

> **"***The Line of Choice distinguishes between a mindset of achieving results versus giving reasons for why a result has not or cannot be achieved.***"**

with discipline. It needs to be a conscious principle that one undertakes daily.

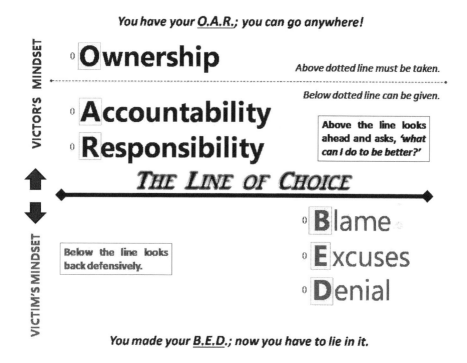

My personal awareness for the *Line of Choice* over the last twelve plus years (encompassing my business coaching career), has focused on influencing people to recognize that every decision is a decision of choice. When I look at a total community, I believe that no more than ten percent consistently live out the Line of Choice in an above the line manner. Everyone at some time will fall below the line, such as an unexpected death of a loved one, or a traumatic situation. The critical mindset is being able to recognize the unexpected fall below the line and to take proactive action to revert to an above the line mindset. *To the extent that I can influence others to*

be aware of whether they are acting above or below the line, I feel that I can help people to perform better and be better.

> "I am not a product of my circumstances. I am a product of my decisions"
>
> ~Stephen Covey, Author

2. The Road of Life

Life's road has potholes, detours, and distractions. I recognized early that I needed to deal with a problem when it occurred; immediately, not later. Problems don't go away . . . they only get bigger. From a 'tap, tap,' on the shoulder, a problem can quickly become a two-by-four; the problem becomes much more difficult to deal with and to correct. If you don't deal with the two-by-four (or four-by-two for my Australian friends), it becomes a Mack Truck with traumatic results. It is absolutely necessary—at the point of awareness of a problem—to take care of it at that time no matter how difficult the issue appears to be.

I call this principle *the road of life* because it applies to anything personal, professional, or spiritual; this principle applies every time. Its universal application doesn't make it easy. To correct a problem at the tap-tap stage, in its own right, is most likely already the beginning of a potential conflict.

ooooooooo

Failure to deal with confrontation....it's an excuse.

By Iain Macfarlane in the Capital Region Business Journal, Madison, Wisconsin

One of the most critical elements I have found in the business world that prevents people from achieving greatness is ignoring problems at the "tap-tap" stage...the initial stage when the person knows, or at least senses, that a conflict exists.

It doesn't matter who you are - business owner, corporate executive, CEO, parent, teenager, social worker, celebrity or everyday person - you can't reach your full potential unless you learn to deal with and quickly rid yourself of the fear of confrontation in conflict resolution.

A great number of people who do not deal with problematic situations in their business or personal lives develop a tendency to bury their emotions. In their own mind, they may believe they have not only addressed the problems but they have dealt with them, but burying emotions is a short-term solution that rarely solves anything.

What those people are really doing is developing a bad habit. They are still not dealing with the core of the complication and, over time, the quick-fix solution can manifest trouble of its own and lead to more extreme confrontational situations.

It's like getting hit by a two-by-four because you did not deal with the problem at the "tap-tap" stage; worse yet, delaying the two-by-four stage would be like getting hit by a big truck.

When you run from your problems, they only get bigger. If you find yourself reacting to another person over the simplest problem in a frustrated, angry, defensive, distant manner, or you find yourself trying to escape by indulging in vices, it is most likely because of a past situation that has not been resolved. It's possible that you have become so used to a problem that you may not even be aware of why you are reacting in a particular way.

Why would you avoid a situation in which you differ from another person? Perhaps you feel insecure or intimidated by certain people when you disagree with them or when they confront you. It may make you uneasy to see other people emotionally upset, crying, or talking loudly. Nonetheless, differences and confrontations are a part of life and they occur in every business. How should you start to deal with confrontation? Consider some suggestions on handling difficult conversations and respond to emotionally charged situations.

ooooooooo

Don't be afraid of confrontation. Too many people become agitated out of fear when they encounter conflict or disagreement. This is unfortunate, as confrontation and conflict are a part of nature, a part of life. Unless you are a hermit, odds are you will have run into confrontational situations, as they are inescapable in business and personal life.

Move to a private setting. Most people do not want an audience when discussing a problem that has upset them. Go to a place without the distraction and concern of uninvolved parties.

Don't blow up; don't clam up; open up! Open up communication. Anger is not bad; it is what you do with it that is right or wrong. Anger just means that you are not happy with a situation. In your opinion, there is something that is not right, and it needs to be addressed. There are two negative reactions stemming from anger that shut down the communication: blowing up and clamming up. When people "vent" and yell and raise their voice, it shuts down the communication. No one listens to a hot head, and no one likes to be yelled at or criticized. There is another response to anger that can also cut off the communication: clamming up. When a person sulks, holds grudges or just refuses to talk, the problem does not get addressed. Both reactions prevent dealing with the core issue. Instead, you need to speak your mind clearly, but with kindness and gentleness and in consideration of the other person's feelings.

Avoid negative or confrontational language. Rather than "buts" and "you're wrongs," try using positive language that disarms rather than confronts, such as: "I understand your position..." or "I can see your point and here is where I'm coming from ..." Although war is part of our nature, most successful societies have been built on cooperation. Common goals are great unifiers. How many stories have you heard of strangers acting together in times of emergency? When a common goal is made obvious, the natural reaction is to put differences aside. Make a mutual commitment to the greater good.

Diffuse emotion by being proactive, not reactive. There is no good reason to respond to an upset person in like kind. It takes two people to argue, and arguments do not solve problems, but instead drive people farther apart. You need to calm down and be in control of your emotions before working on a problem. Thank them for bringing the situation to your attention. You cannot fix what you don't understand. One of the best ways to diffuse anger from another person is to listen to them.

Much anger and frustration stems from people feeling misunderstood, ignored or not cared for. **Seek first to understand and only then to be understood.** This principle is habit number five of Stephen Covey's well-respected, *"7 Habits of Highly Effective People."* To paraphrase how it has worked in my own life, the idea is to get a complete understanding of the problem from the other person's viewpoint, and then repeat that understanding back to him or her in your own words. Once you have restated that person's perspective in your own words, ask whether you have a correct understanding. Ask the other person to do the same.

Attack the problem, not the person. Once you have a clear understanding of the problem, look for areas of agreement before addressing the differences. Then you will have a basis to find solutions and resolutions where you differ. Often, just listening and understanding each other will resolve a problem. Invite the other person to help you find a solution.

Look for win/win resolutions. Find out clearly what the other person wants, and clearly state what you want. Then work together to find a mutually satisfactory solution. There are many ways to solve any problem. Be innovative and creative. If necessary, find an outside mediator whom you both trust to facilitate the communication and a solution. In reality, you should abandon the concept of winning and losing. Instead, when faced with conflict, adopt a strategy of resolution. Unless you are on a battlefield, chances are the person you come into conflict with is not the enemy, but instead is someone whose goals are generally similar to yours, or at least interrelated to yours.

Consider talking through the situation with a neutral party to gain perspective and clarity from that person, and also to better understand the conflict. It is helpful to get a problem out in the open and to get input from people you trust. They can help you better understand what you are going through and tell you, for better or worse, whether they think you have properly judged or handled the situation.

Be flexible. Rather than approaching the conflict with the attitude of stopping it or overcoming it, think of redirecting the energy toward a common target. Look for similarities in your positions rather than focusing on your differences. When the other side senses that you are interested in finding a solution, you likely will have created an ally where a potential adversary once stood. Rather than confrontation and conflict, you can cooperate to find a solution that suits both sides.

ooooooooo

- When it comes to confrontations, you need to approach confrontation as an expected part of dealing with others.
- Consider confrontation as a way of learning to see issues more clearly.
- Deal with confrontation immediately when you know or sense the "tap-tap."
- Don't wait to be hit by a two-by-four or, even worse, by a big truck.

3. <u>The Platinum Rule of Communications</u>

The famous "golden rule," dating back to the Book of Matthew in the New Testament of the Holy Bible, written in approximately the year 70, has always been to treat others as you would like to be treated. It's certainly a positive sentiment. In recent years, though, sociological, behavioral and cultural insights and assessments have proven that the way others want to be treated or communicated to may be entirely different from how we want to be treated or communicated to. The Platinum Rule goes beyond the Golden Rule by accommodating the unique feelings of others. It is the principle of treating and communicating to others the way they want to be treated or communicated to.

Enter DISC theory, developed by William Moulton Marston in the early twentieth century. DISC theory identifies behavioral characteristics including Dominant, Influencing, Steady, or Compliant. While the DISC behavioral assessments break down desires, motivators, behaviors, and inter-relational styles in much greater detail than these four basic words, DISC highlights the fact that not everybody will respond to the same communication in the same way. Dr. Tony Alessandra uses DISC to enforce what he deemed "The Platinum Rule" (TPR). Treat others the way THEY want to be treated; communicate with and treat others as THEY wish; connect and flex to others recognizing that everyone you communicate with will be different.

" *. . . sociological, behavioral, and cultural insights and assessments have proven that the way others want to be treated or communicated to may be entirely different from how we want to be treated or communicated to.* "

TPR takes DISC to its next level of functionality. When I was at the East-West Center from 1962-1964, I quickly learned that I had to adjust in order to communicate effectively – in a way that was responsive to the other person. It was more important for me to understand each person's culture rather than their language; students came from almost every country in Asia, the Pacific region, and the U.S. I could be a far better communicator by having empathy for the other person's culture than knowledge of their language. Once I displayed empathy and emotion, the responses to my communication could become more open.

When working on Polaroid advertising worldwide from 1978-1980, I had thirty-two different countries communicating with me. Going to a meeting was about respecting the culture. We needed translators, but that was mechanics. Effecting change and influencing was done through empathy and emotion.

In January of 1978, Polaroid had taken American commercials and translated them into the foreign language. The classic example to look at was Japan, the second largest market for Polaroid products. American commercials were full of copy – words and explanations. Japanese commercials were more visual and symbolic. Polaroid didn't have a strong rapport in Japan. I led a changed approach to advertising there. Instead of American commercials directly translated to become *linguistically* Japanese, we created entirely new advertising that was *culturally* Japanese. The commercials had very few words, but lots of colors and visual representation. Following this change of communication style, adapting to the way the Japanese people wanted to be communicated to, there was a significant increase in sales.

How do you express thoughts that have a cultural impact, rather than a linguistic one?

We also learned to grasp onto the Japanese affection for celebrity for those American commercials that could still culturally reach some attraction in the Japanese market. For instance, there was an American commercial to launch the One-Step Camera which starred James Garner. See *"Time Zero One-Step."* https://www.youtube.com/watch?v=WsjdMv9qyoU *(Or scan the QR code.)*

At the time of the commercial, Mariette Hartley was an out-of-work, single mom. We hired her to be a female counter (but interactive personality) with James Garner, doing a few commercials in the U.S. It was so powerful, that we contracted her for two years to develop more commercials with James Garner. The two worked together so well (and naturally on set), that they only had to have the concept from the copywriters; from there, they improvised and developed it to create very believable and effective situations. Those commercials, with translated voiceovers, also worked in Japan because of the celebrity culture and because the characters who connected emotions to the technical product.

4. Formula for Change

Why is change so difficult? Why does change hold back so many people from doing things they know they should do? Why is the grip of one's comfort zone so binding?

It was the Greek philosopher, Heraclitus, around 500 BC, who first said, "The only thing that is constant is change." Given the nature of the famous words of wisdom, it's no surprise that his quotation has also remained constant some two and a half millennia later. If personally or professionally you choose to stand in place, while the rest of the world moves forward around you, it will appear to others that you are moving backwards. It's a necessary principle of life to accept and embrace change, find ways to adapt with the change, and discover how to grow comfortable with the adaptation.

When outside of your comfort zone, the formula for change requires, above all, recognition or feelings of some Dissatisfaction (D) with current circumstances, as well as a Vision (V) for something greater than your dissatisfaction, and to have a reason or a need for Urgency (U). Beyond that recognition and thought process, the person can only be able to initiate the change process by identifying a First step (F) to that change. In many cases taking the first step will seem to be overwhelming. In those situations my guidance is to find a person who can provide a Support structure (S) to begin the change process and to continue to monitor achieving the results that represent the desired change. IF, after all of those pieces of the formula are identified and put into practice, THEN resistance (R) to change is overcome. As resistance is overcome, an individual's natural desire to stay in his or her comfort zone is also overcome and positive change can occur.

Remind yourself of this formula and apply it as a driver to make decisions about change and to move outside your comfort zone through conscious use of this equation:

$$(D \times V \times U) + (F \times S) > R = \textbf{\underline{CHANGE}}$$

Everyone has a level of dissatisfaction over different parts of life, personal or professional. The reason why change is so difficult is that people tend to get stuck at the Vision piece of the formula. They create vision as what they already know and are comfortable with rather than create a forward-looking picture in their lives. The detail sought and necessary in the Vision step of the formula for change is: a Vision for something greater than your Dissatisfaction . . . to happen. If it has not yet happened, it is yet to come – in the future. This future-looking is critical to completing the formula for change and, in order to develop that future picture, it's vital to absorb and apply the fifth driver for life success, The PRESENT-FUTURE Mindset.

5. <u>PRESENT-FUTURE</u> Mindset

Saving the most important driver for last, I'll introduce you to the PRESENT-FUTURE Mindset, in the next chapter. I didn't always have a PRESENT-FUTURE Mindset, meaning: *a mindset that uses present circumstances to visualize and predict future realities,* in order to make decisions. In reflection, however, this mindset has truly become the principal driver in all aspects of my life.

*"PRESENT-FUTURE Mindset is
a mindset that uses present
circumstances to visualize and
predict future realities, in order
to make a decision."*

~I.M.

The Power of the Fifth Driver

. . . So You Can Create the Future Picture

"Winners learn from the past and enjoy working in the present toward the future."

~Denis Waitley, Writer and Motivational Speaker

*I*t's natural for people to live in a Past-Present Mindset; it is the comfort zone for most people. We live in that mindset every day of our lives in the majority of the actions we take in those lives. *How do I get to work?* The same way I've driven there every day. *How do I prepare a cup of coffee?* No differently than I did the day before. These aren't things we think about doing; they are habits; we just do them. However, in our brains, a process is taking place.

1. **Identify a problem:** I need to get to work.
2. **Explore options:** I could take the train, walk, bike, or drive.
3. **Consider your PAST experience and knowledge:** The weather is not appropriate for walking or biking and my city does not have reliable public transportation.

4. **Choose a solution for the problem:** I have to drive my car to work.

In business, a more pertinent example of how a Past-Present Mindset is often used, is in the decision-making process surrounding the development of an annual budget. Often, the current business direction is extended for the next year. If increases have occurred across a line of business, budgets increase there. If another line of business is faltering, a leader may choose to pull back from that area. This is a narrow-focused approach that doesn't take change, future options, or risk into consideration.

Imagine that, as a team, a business owner leads a SWOT Analysis (identification of **S**.trengths, **W**.eaknesses, **O**.pportunities, and **T**.hreats). Through the SWOT Analysis, he or she discovers that there is an opportunity which—based on the company's strengths—could be sought as a new market. The threat to this opportunity is a competitor who, based on *past* weaknesses, is difficult to compete with in a cost-efficient manner. Using the traditional Past-Present Mindset model, the thinking might continue as such:

1. **Identify a problem:** We have to develop a unique service offering that could exist in the current marketplace.
2. **Explore options:** We could offer at a lower cost to provide a greater value to the client.
3. **Consider your PAST experience and knowledge:** The competitor is large and can therefore reduce costs more easily.

4. **Choose a solution for the problem:** The time is not right for the new service line to be launched successfully.

When basing decisions on past knowledge, there tends to be a dislike for risk-taking; however, it is in the risk-taking that innovation takes place and success can be achieved at the greatest rate. A future-looking leader might have developed value through a completely remodeled offering, different from that of the competitor (taking a *changing* market into consideration). While many leaders recognize and accept the risk to reward relationship, even the most creative among us find it difficult to think *outside* of what is concrete fact and proven experience and—by its very definition—this is something that has happen**ed** . . . that is PAST.

A Past-Present Mindset means that the first thoughts to address a problem (or opportunity), or the first thoughts to describe a situation, will be something that already has happened or already is happening. The natural instinct is to deal with problems and opportunities based on what a person already knows and has experienced. Past-Present Mindset reflects something that is definitive and tangible in the person's mind. It's much more comfortable to be able to relate to something already known. The Past-Present Mindset allows us to live in our comfort zones.

There are some positives to the Past-Present Mindset. It provides a foundational base of knowledge. It's not negative to revert to existing knowledge; the critical factor is that the past is being recognized as such and it won't change going forward to provide a solution or even an understanding of something new or different . . . *unless one chooses to do something about it!*

A Past-Present Mindset could prove negative, though, when used as the primary reason to do things in the future. *Past* knowledge should not be used as a direct translation of what *will* occur in the future, either.

Going back to the example problem of, "I need to get to work," what would happen if there were construction along the usual driving route? Would the person simply not go to work at all? What if a rideshare or reliable transportation became available that freed up time for the worker to read, make calls, or listen to professional development audio books? Shouldn't that be grounds for considering a change?

It's easy to see the absurdity of locking into a Past-Present Mindset for such a simple example. Unfortunately many leaders and entrepreneurs live there for decisions and actions, such as the budgeting scenario shared. Those decisions and actions have genuine consequences and those leaders watch their brand (and their legacies) fade away as a result of living in the past, their comfort zone.

One need not look too far in the past or away from our everyday realities to see a commercial collateral damage from the Past-Present Mindset. Take Blockbuster, for instance; it was founded in 1985 as, primarily, a movie rental franchise organization. As a company, they managed to move from video cassettes to DVDs and eventually even added gaming to their offerings. The *model* didn't change, though, and they ultimately made the decision not to enter the world of streamlining. With an already existent customer-base of movie lovers, they could have become the next Netflix, Hulu, or

Amazon Instant Video. *To continue to grow and to be successful, we must have a mindset to rethink, rebuild, or take an unknown route.* Knowledge of the past is rarely indicative of results in the future.

In my college days I used to feel that, just by knowing what the existing problems of the world were, and understanding and analyzing issues like poverty, malnourishment, the wealth gap, etc., I could fix the world. It was overwhelming and this Past-Present Mindset actually led to accepting the situation as it historically had been rather than visualizing and focusing on what could be done about it in a PRESENT-FUTURE Mindset.

What opportunities could be lurking out there in your life and left unexplored because of a Past-Present Mindset?

DOs of a Past-Present Mindset

- o Do use a Past-Present Mindset to gain knowledge.
- o Do use a Past-Present Mindset to consider options based on historical experience.

DON'Ts of a Past-Present Mindset

- o Don't allow a Past-Present Mindset to prevent you from trying something new.
- o Don't allow a Past-Present Mindset to prevent you from growth; i.e., from visualizing what you want your life to be like.
- o Don't allow a Past-Present Mindset to bias you toward different options that may be out of date related to new products.
- o Don't allow a Past-Present Mindset to overwhelm you into accepting the unacceptable.

The PRESENT-FUTURE Mindset first became apparent to me in my professional life a short time after I joined Power.Base Systems in New York City in 1984, in the early days of the new desktop computer wave. Power.Base was a desktop database system competing with DBaseII from Ashton Tate. The technology inventor of Power.Base had been running the company on behalf of venture capitalists; unfortunately, like so many inventors who start and manage their own companies from launch, he was failing as a business person in the business growth phase. I was recruited by the controlling Venture Capital firms, J.H. Whitney and Oak Management, to turnaround Power.Base.

I spent the first month talking to already contacted potential customers to understand why they were not buying Power.Base, even after the product had been demonstrated as a clearly superior and easier product to use.

At the first monthly Board meeting, I presented the prior month's financials as usual. The Venture Capitalists said to me, "We can read those numbers as well as you; we want to know where we'll be at the end of the year."

In the second month, I still spent my time in the marketplace identifying our business problem. At the second monthly Board meeting, I again presented the prior month's and year-to-date financial reports. This time, the Venture Capitalists again made it clear that they could *still* read those numbers just as well as me. Their emphatic question was, *"WHAT WILL WE LOOK LIKE AT THE END OF THE YEAR?"*

That moment was an epiphany for me. I needed to find a way to forecast the end of the year. The real value of a PRESENT-FUTURE Mindset was—as a business person—to be able to make assumptions about where the company would be in the future. The numbers would be based on assumptions and these assumptions would be informed assumptions using information I was getting from the marketplace.

As much as I had my first applicable understanding of the value of a PRESENT-FUTURE Mindset as a necessary element of building business in 1984, the principle of PRESENT-FUTURE Mindset has become more of a concrete, fundamental thought process through my broader experience of working with a range of businesses where I held CEO roles, as well as working with clients in different industries through my coaching of the past twelve years.

As much as the PRESENT-FUTURE Mindset formally evolved from business experiences, I have now come to realize that it's a fundamental principle that applies to all of life. Moreover, I eventually recognized its origins in my life through some international educational and travel experiences, in the 1960s.

I began to discover and recognize the importance of life's experiences to define drivers, and principles to create and visualize my future legacy, with the PRESENT-FUTURE Mindset at the heart of it all.

"I have now come to realize that the PRESENT-FUTURE Mindset is the fundamental principle that applies to all of life."

~I.M.

The Power of East, West, and Finding Center

... So You Can Define Your Purpose

"The boldness of asking deep questions may require unforeseen flexibility if we are to accept the answers."

~Brian Greene, American Theoretical Physicist

*L*ong before my experience with Power.Base Systems, when I was absorbing the experiences that would ultimately bring clarity years later, I was given an opportunity that would lead me on a path toward PRESENT-FUTURE Mindset and toward my chosen legacy. After four years at Sydney University, living the typical collegiate life of sports, working hard, taking a flat mate to share the rent, studying hard, (and still finding ways to fit in girls and the occasional prank with a friend), a new door opened.

In September of 1962, I arrived, as a Fellow, at the East-West Center (EWC) in Honolulu; it had been established in 1960 by U.S. leadership under the guidance of the Senator Lyndon Johnson. He wanted to build better connections between young future leaders in the rapidly growing Asia and Pacific region of the world. The East-West Center was to be a post-graduate organization for cultural and technical interchange between Asia, the Pacific and the United States. The EWC campus adjoined the University of Hawaii where the EWC students attended for traditional academic studies.

The EWC campus was still under construction when I first arrived in Honolulu; the first four buildings were designed by the world famous architect I.M. Pei. The EWC is now recognized as one of the foremost programs in the world for Asia-Pacific studies. *(Learn about this highly-respected international organization at www.eastwestcenter.org or scan the QR code.)*

For the first few months after arrival, until the Men's dormitory was opened in January of 1963, I was put into a dormitory at a Buddhist Temple and my roommate, by coincidence, was a Thai Buddhist. My religious/spiritual background was narrow, so I asked a lot of questions in coming to know him and his background and beliefs. My roommate's values came from a more philosophical and spiritual belief system than one that was traditionally religious (in my own context). I understood, for the first time, how differently people believed and thought.

One of the most eye-opening experiences I had was getting to know a Japanese man who had been a young officer in a submarine in World War II—an "enemy" submarine officer. I thought of the HMAS Sydney and my father's mission after the loss of 645 Australian Sailors. I became a boy again; I was brought back in my mind to my childhood fears of invasion as I watched the flickering flashes of curtains and shadows rustling in the breeze at the home of my mother's cousin. The innocent fear paralysis was vivid in my mind. From that Japanese veteran's perspective, though, he was merely trained for the work he did.

"We did what we were told," he said to me.

'Was that really any different than my own father, or uncles, or aunts?' He loved his country as I loved my own.

The two of us eventually became good friends, particularly over a few beers. I imagine it was even harder for him to make friends at the East-West Center. He was a World War II Japanese man taking up residence in the Pearl Harbor state. My friendship with him was the first time that I realized all of the life lessons I'd already experienced had been building me as a person. I thought about my relationships with Aboriginal children who were considered outcasts in my own country and I came to respect the intercultural blindness with which I didn't even realize I'd been brought up. I was beginning to gain awareness of my own identity.

East-West Center students on a Maui beach after National Country presentations to the Maui community and high schools.

The EWC's programming made certain we had a good deal of activities to do together to encourage our interchange. There were students from more than thirty nationalities and there were only two of us from Australia. Connecting meant connecting with these "strangers," culturally, socially, and politically and knowing that we were all foreign to one another; we had to find our commonalities in our humanity.

Keeping to his wandering Aussie roots, Iain often explored while at the EWC. Here he is in 1964 hiking in the Valley to the Lost Tribes of Kauai.

I began to have an understanding of true differences. We celebrated one another's holidays. We all participated in one another's lives. We put on shows and programs that represented our unique cultures. Saturday nights were cultural events. I remember Korean dancers, Indian singers, and Hawaiian hula.

'How do you represent Australia on a stage,' the other fellow Aussie and I wondered. When our turn came up, we put on a skit of sorts. We acted as two Australians sharing stories, chock full of our native slang in a thick Aussie dialect over beers in a pub at the end of a work day – the typical lifestyle of most Aussies! All of the EWC students spoke English as a requirement, but no one, including the Americans who spoke English as their native language, could understand a word that Dennis and I said – we were a 'foreign' language culture. When we brought our native country culture programs into schools and communities, I replaced this

Scan for Iain's reading of "The Man from Snowy River" on the ERH.

skit with a reading of Australia's epic poem, *"The Man from Snowy River,"* By Banjo Patterson, my personal favorite poem.

Once again coming full-circle, readings of "The Man from Snowy River" brought back memories of his Australian raising. Above, see Iain, at age four, on a horse at his Great Uncle's sheep farm in Piawaning, Western Australia.

ooooooo

While at the EWC, I: experienced the thirteen-day Cuban Missile Crisis in October of 1962 just one month after my arrival in the U.S.; feared through the tsunami sirens that followed the Great Alaskan Earthquake in March of 1964 when some coastal damage occurred in Hawaii; represented Indonesia on behalf of the State of Hawaii at the five-day Model United Nations for college students held in San Jose, California in March 1963; spent a required semester in another country (for me—as an Australian—this was New York's Columbia University); took a trip to Mexico where—in the midst of Montezuma's revenge—I would meet my future wife, Madge; mourned the assassination of John F. Kennedy while I was on U.S. soil in New York City; undertook a 9000 plus-mile, nationwide tour of the U.S., mostly on Continental Trailways buses, to do a research project on "The application of computers in the American Steel Industry"; was called (as a white man) on one occasion, during the 1963 summer of civil rights rioting, to sit in the front of a bus before the driver would leave; felt my first ever snowfall in upstate New York while visiting friends . . . it never occurred to me that snow would be wet, rather than soft; traveled back to Hawaii for the final Semester of my East-West Center program; had my first (of three) brushes with the CIA; went on educational visits to the Outer Islands of Hawaii; and built bonds of friendship as unlikely as those of a four-year-old, white, shepherd boy and neighboring, outcasted, Aboriginal children.

ooooooo

The EWC gave me a worldly understanding and world sharing. All of the experiences were incredibly emotional and this was the place where I learned that culture was the most important part of understanding others.

(Read about cultural awareness in communication at https://goo.gl/LxEYgvor scan the QR code.)

"Culture was the most important part of understanding others."

Decades later, the experiences obtained at the birth of this great, international, intercultural, social, academic experiment still affect the way I live my life and the way I coach others toward their own legacies.

At left: 40ᵗʰ East-West Center Reunion, Honolulu, 2002. Iain is nearest to the bus door.

After my experience at the East-West Center, I now had a wide breadth of knowledge. I had cognitive understanding of a great deal of information across many cultures. I even had awareness, or at least a better understanding of how my own life experiences had shaped my own emotions, thoughts, words, and actions. After an experience with so much worldly influence, I didn't find my thirst for knowledge and awareness shrinking. I was hungry for more. That hunger would lead me to the seven month trip through parts of Asia and India. The trip commenced after completing my two years at the East-West Center and it brought the fullness of my newly learned skills by adding new applications to my knowledge and awareness.

oooooooo

Because of the Japanese student I'd become friends with at the EWC, my childhood fears of the nation had been broken down. My mind had been opened. Following my completion of the EWC studies in May 1964, I had one experience I'll never forget.

I decided to visit Japan.

On a ship en route from Honolulu to Yokohama, Japan, I met up with a United States Green Beret who had served in the early days of Vietnam. We became good, quick friends on the ship. He was about to spend six months in Tokyo to get his black belt in Aikido Martial Arts.

Left: Iain's Green Beret friend, John, upon arriving in Tokyo. Above: businessmen and workers play "GO" at lunch in a Tokyo, Japan street, 1964

When we arrived in Japan, we ended up together at the Tokyo International House, an inexpensive place to stay that had strict accommodation rules such as doors closed (and locked) at nine o'clock P.M. After a couple of nights of coming back to International House at this early hour, we ended up unlocking a third floor window and opted to scale our way up to the unlocked window (knowing that we wanted to come back much later than 9:00 P.M.). It worked once, then twice. On the third night, we scaled up at one or two o'clock in the morning - the windows had been locked!

We went to a park bench across the street. We got woken up with a flashlight in our faces by a police officer. We couldn't speak much Japanese, but we understood that we were told to stay there. I assumed we were going to be arrested. The police officer came back and had blankets for us.

In that moment, my transition was complete. I really, truly had changed my total mindset on Japan from Past-Preset to PRESENT-FUTURE.

After a few more days of sight-seeing Tokyo, I went off on my own by local trains to Kyoto and Nara, where a person can learn all of the ancient, traditional ways of life in Japan, including the influence of the Samurai. Then I continued onto Hiroshima. It was an incredible experience. In those days, less than twenty years after the end of World War II, many people still wore Kimonos and other traditional attire. Women kept coming up to me and shouting at me, "B-52s, B-52s! You kill!"

Below: Hiroshima Memorial, 1964

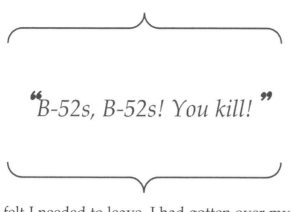

"B-52s, B-52s! You kill!"

Iain Macfarlane

I was a tall, white man in this area deliberately untouched from the impact of the atomic bomb and I couldn't speak their language. I felt I needed to leave. I had gotten over my personal fears but I was "attacking" theirs.

From Japan, I began a five plus month-long trek of the truly undeveloped world of Asia that I emotionally, perhaps even desperately, wanted to "fix."

ooooooooo

The Trip that Defined the Legacy

Where: *Hong Kong*

What I saw: An active, vibrant city in a British colony; I saw Hong Kong already starting major building construction.

What I thought: I recognized Hong Kong as a rapidly growing trade center.

ooooooooo

Where: *Macau*

What I saw: It was a poor, decrepit Portuguese colonial trading port and nowhere near as vibrant as Hong Kong.

What I thought: This was extreme poverty; I only stayed a day.

ooooooo

Where: *Manila, Philippines*

What I saw: More real poverty. . . and I was taking it in as a *sightseer* which felt disconnecting to me.

What I thought: They had a difficult situation with their large, overcrowded city population.

ooooooo

My trip by ship, which began in Japan, then ended in Singapore. My Australian grandparents had lived there at the turn of the twentieth century. My grandfather had been the Harbor Master. I stayed with family friends who showed me a great time. It was an historical and personal stop for me, as were my next few visits through South-East Asia. First, I went by train to Kuala Lumpur where my Dad had worked; and then to Penang where my Mum had worked as a High School teacher after her first period as a High School teacher in Phuket, Thailand.

Singapore, 1964; today, a contemporary city

Penang is where my parents met. My father before the war was a Managing Agent for a Scottish company that handled the properties of wealthy, absentee owners (primarily rubber plantations). He had been transferred from Aberdeen, Scotland, where he grew up. He first went to Burma, then Borneo and finally to Kuala Lumpur (near Penang).

The next leg of the trip took me by train (third class) to Bangkok. As my roommate at the EWC, Praphon Jearakul was from Thailand and as my mother had told me wonderful stories about her time in Thailand (Phuket and Bangkok), I was really looking forward to this part of my trip and also knowing that I was going to spend time with friends.

The floating market in Bangkok, shown in these photos from 1964, no longer exists

In 1964 Thailand was my picture of the exotic "Far East".

Crowded, bustling, river

markets, great food and dramatic, colorful Temples throughout the city. I stayed in the family home of the Headmaster of the High School my mother had taught at in Phuket. Because the headmaster's family was related to the Royal Family of Thailand, I certainly had the chance to see the best of Thai life.

1964 Border Crossing from Thailand to Cambodia

Where: *Cambodia*

I didn't have much money. I took the train to the border of Thailand and Cambodia. I had learned quite a few card tricks earlier in life and I found the Thai people loved gambling. I got on the train without a ticket and took a chance on getting there literally by luck. I was doing tricks when the conductor came by and by involving him in the tricks he allowed me a free ride to the border of Cambodia. At this border crossing there were no immigration officials or border crossing buildings on either side of the border – I just walked into Cambodia! From there, I went on local busses and walking to various destinations.

Above: a family in Cambodia, 1964
At right: water buffalo play in the waters in front of Angkor Wat, 1964

Nature reclaimed this Angkor Wat temple; a Wonder of the World; here it is in 1964

What I saw: A main center of Cambodia was Angkor Wat (the old capitol of the Khmer civilization). It was deep in the jungle and, at that time, recently discovered. It's an incredible city that was built of stone in the twelfth Century.

Angkor Wat has been called one of the Wonders of the World with impressiveness, by some opinions, that is greater than that of the Pyramids with artistic distinctiveness as fine as that of the Taj Mahal.

It was originally built as a Hindu funerary temple. Then, in the Sixteenth Century, it became a Buddhist monument and was cared for by Buddhist monks. In 1964 when I visited Angkor Wat there were less than five thousand tourists per year; in 2015 there were over two million tourists!

What I thought: I was overwhelmed in thinking about the way of life over many previous centuries as I toured the

massive grounds and buildings riding an elephant.

Left: Iain on the back of an elephant in Angkor Wat. He's pictured here in the attire he donned for his entire Asian/Indian trip of 1964.

I left Angkor Wat in an attempt to get to Phnom Penh, the capitol of Cambodia, as my next destination only to find it was a high risk place to go to because of the proximity to the Vietnam War. I decided to return to Bangkok; again no border check between Cambodia back into Thailand.

ooooooo

*A Chiang Mai,
Thailand street and
market, 1964*

Where: Thailand, *Bangkok to Chiang Mai and the North-West Border with Burma and Laos ('The Golden Triangle')*

What I saw: A rural Thai city in spectacular, scenic mountainous country and beautiful Buddhist temples. I stayed with my Mother's friend from her days in Phuket who was the newly appointed Chancellor for the opening of Chiang Mai University and I also met with him and the head of education for the United Nations who was visiting this new university in a remote part of South-East Asia.

What I thought: This area was known worldwide as "The Golden Triangle" of drugs, and specifically opium and heroin (Thailand, Burma, and Laos); it was perhaps the largest illegal narcotic drug production area in the world. I was personally shocked to be exposed to the dramatic contrast of the natural beauty of this part of the world and the massive destruction to human life across the world caused by the hard drugs that came from this area.

ooooooooo

Where: *Burma (now Myanmar) – Rangoon (now Yangon)*

Flew from Bangkok to Rangoon for three days on a very restricted Visa (Rangoon only) as few foreigners could visit Burma in the 1960s. At this time, flying was the only way in or out of Burma for foreigners.

> **"***I was personally shocked to be exposed to the dramatic contrast of the natural beauty of this part of the world and the massive destruction to human life across the world caused by the drugs that came from this area.* **"**

What I saw: The scenery and temples were beautiful.

What I thought: It was an ancient Buddhist country with some equally ancient (and somewhat backward) ways of living.

The Schwedagon Pagoda, Burma, pictured here in 1964, is one of the last scenes Iain would capture before his entire mindset changed through his Asian/Indian trip.

Where: Chittagong, East Pakistan (now independent as Bangladesh)

What I saw: Extreme poverty of the people, rubbish lying everywhere, people (and animals) malnourished and buildings dilapidated and in poor condition. Everything seemed even worse when severe monsoon rainstorms pounded down at frequent intervals every day I was there.

Chittagong – East Pakistan (Bangladesh) 1964

What I thought: I had never seen anything like this and I had no idea that conditions of life could be this bad and I'm sure disease was rampant.

ooooooooo

India was a journey in itself...

> "*This was the beginning of the personally most impactful three months of my trip—perhaps of my life....*"

I arrived in Calcutta from Chittagong by plane and found a Salvation Army dormitory for accommodation; based on my first emotional reaction to the destitute conditions of the area I assumed I was in a very poor neighborhood. This was the beginning of the personally most impactful three months of my trip—perhaps of my life—seeing ways of life from rich to poor that I would not have believed if I had not seen them with my own eyes; three months of 'hitch-hiking' on transport trucks, local buses, third class trains, a DC-3 plane flight and even on a bullock wagon

ooooooo

Where: Calcutta (now Kolkata):

What I saw: On my first night in a Salvation Army Hostel, the temperature and humidity were extremely high (monsoon season) and I was unable to sleep in the un-air conditioned dormitory. By three o'clock in the morning, I decided to get up and go for a walk in the street. What a shock. There were people lying side-by-side on every sidewalk, some covered with cloth and many covered by no more than newspaper. An hour later, it even got worse. Men

> **"***A dead body was lifted onto wagons being pushed on the street to collect the bodies—not one, not five, not ten—but many, many dead bodies.***"**

began walking down the sidewalks, prodding bodies with a

stick to determine who was dead. A dead body was lifted onto wagons being pushed on the street to collect the bodies—not one, not five, not ten—but many, many dead bodies. I could not eat or sleep for the next two days and nights.

Worse realizations were to come. I asked for some guidance for site seeing. The number one recommendation, 'the pride of Calcutta', was the Queen Victoria Memorial (palace) from the British colonial days. It was a massive, magnificent, white building set in beautiful fenced and guarded grounds (and as striking as the Taj Mahal that I was to see later in my trip). The contrast of the degradation on the streets to the opulence of the Queen Victoria Memorial was incomprehensible to the point of emotionally painful.

The contrast between (above) Queen Victoria's Memorial Palace and the streets (left) of Calcutta was sickening and emotionally painful.

What I thought: After three days in Calcutta, the most devastating poverty I'd ever witnessed, I was starting to understand that it wasn't my job to change people the way my own previous idyllic thoughts had influenced me. If people didn't reach out in some manner, I couldn't force 'idealistic' change upon them. This was their way of life and they were in acceptance of it. I didn't want to impose my thoughts and my mind in telling others how to live. Individuals and groups of people needed to make their own decisions to change. I needed to find a way to offer alternatives so that they could choose on their own.

I was coming to a clear resolution in my own mind. There were certain paths to overcoming trials:

1 – No matter what, people have to make their own choices and some of them had done so;

2 - People can be dependent on others and change through government, but that is always going to be slow, regimented, and political;

3 - Life can change through choices offered from the private sector.

In this part of the world I was taking in, Gandhi brought about change through his individual efforts as a movement's leader, even though he was unwanted at the political level. To make change in that slow, political manner, you must be one with the people and I never would be. I already recognized that the choice for a better life for these people was not mine to make; that same recognition also lies with individual people. My choice was to be part of offering change through a private sector career and it was confirmation of my choice to join H.J. Heinz, the food manufacturing company based in Pittsburgh, Pennsylvania in the U.S. I had a new purpose in my decision to join the private sector after completing my seven month trip through Asia.

oooooooo

Where: Calcutta to Patna, India to Kathmandu, Nepal

Iain's truck ride from Calcutta to Patna

What I saw: To travel the approximate 300 miles from Calcutta to Patna, the second largest city in Northeast India, I met with trucking companies and was able to arrange a ride for the two day/one night trip. The two drivers were Sikhs who spoke no English. Yet we somehow were able to communicate. At one point, a few hundred yards ahead, another truck had run over a pedestrian; our drivers wound their windows up and accelerated past the crowd, as it became obvious the angry crowd could take over our truck; it didn't take English to understand what the drivers were doing.

That evening, we made a stop overnight at a rest area: mud hut, open fire cooking, a well for water and washing, and cots made of vine stresses. In preparation for my trip before leaving Honolulu, I had fourteen injections to help protect against as many possible diseases. On the whole trip the only time I drank any form of water was after boiling and adding a chlorine tablet. The exposure to water and insects at this overnight stop was going to test all of those injections. At sunrise we got up, were given a sheet to put over our heads as we washed our bodies at the well, using our sheets for modesty and protection from the elements.

An overnight stop for Iain en route to Patna

After arrival in Patna I took a local bus to the airport and bought a ticket to Kathmandu, the capitol of Nepal. The plane was a pre-World War II DC3 and not only did we take on human passengers, we also had two goats and a number of chickens! That was not the scary part. As the plane 'lumbered' up into the Himalayan mountains, we passed between ridges and down through valleys; I swear we only had about fifty feet on either side of each wingtip as we went through ridges and I definitely thought my trip was going to end prematurely.

"I definitely thought my trip was going to end prematurely."

On arriving in Kathmandu I had moved from what felt like a way overpopulated Hindu society to a quiet and peaceful Buddhist society in a spectacular setting of valleys and snow capped mountains (and this was the middle of summer). I made a one-day round-trip on the back of a truck with workmen going to and from Bhadgaon (now Bhaktapur), an earlier capitol of Nepal and known as 'the place of devotees'.

Left: a Kathmandu barber
Above: A family in the streets
of Kathmandu

Left: My hitched ride with a
truckload of workers on the
way to Bhadgaon

Above; a house on a hill in Nepal
Below: a Nepal mountain view

After three days in the Kathmandu area, I arranged for a ride on a truck back to the Indian border. We arrived near midnight and I still had to walk three miles to the border crossing and I knew that I could catch a 6:00 A.M. train the next morning. As I began to walk a driver and bullock wagon pulled up beside me and offered me a ride to the border. At about 3:00 A.M. I walked through the border at Birgunj back into India with no one on duty at this point (a little different to security at national borders today!).

What I thought: As I had come to such a powerful self-understanding back in Calcutta, I had now become comfortable within myself and I was really enjoying every moment as I was getting exposed to new ways of life and cultures. I never could have understood these different lives and peoples if I had not had personal contact and experiences in these diverse and 'foreign' environments. First-hand knowledge is very powerful and can be very influential if you gain it with an open mind.

ooooooooo

Where: Nepal border to Benaras (now Varanasi) to Taj Mahal to Delhi

What I saw: My travel between each of these destinations was third class travel on trains, and all were over crowded. There were often wooden benches for seating (including the overhead luggage rack that was used for seating rather than bags); every corridor was full of people standing or sitting on bags; the toilet was a hole in the floor at the end of each carriage; there was no food or beverage service of any kind. Which carriage you got on and where you sat was a fight at each stop that included more aggressive people climbing through the windows to be onboard first and the latecomers who opted to ride on the roof, rather than miss the train.

> "*Their heads were bound so they didn't grow physically or mentally.*"

Benaras, on the Ganges River, is the most visited pilgrimage destination in India, particularly as the most Holy site for Hindus. I was mesmerized by so much going on that was foreign to me. People were bathing in the river, I witnessed burning funeral pyres and the professional beggars in the streets including pinheads who were led with begging pans. ("Pinheads" were people who had been given as young children to temples for religious purposes and their heads were bound so they didn't grow physically or mentally.) Begging at the time I was in India was a legalized practice tied to religion.

The Taj Mahal in Agra, an ivory-white mausoleum built in the seventeenth century, is one of the wonders of the world and is visually striking. Under a full moon, its splendor is a memory for life. On the opposite side of this wonder, it was difficult to accept the contrast of women making cow dung into patties with their hands, forcing them onto the walls of their houses (huts) to provide fuel for their cooking – I wondered what the smell must have been like in their tiny huts!

In Delhi, I had the opportunity to stay with the parents of one of the Indian students from the East-West Center. Delhi was a cosmopolitan city and I really was only exposed to upper class experiences. Given most of my travel and experiences in India up to that time, I really enjoyed being exposed to the developed, educated, and sophisticated class of India. It was almost a respite from my other travels. Every nation has its own form of cultural and economic classes and I'm glad I also had the exposure to the upper class society in India.

Taj Mahal serves as a shining example of more contrast between extreme wealth and extreme poverty in India

What I thought: Contrast, contrast, and contrast! Between wealth and poverty, between religious power and choice, between food and hunger, between luck and hopelessness, between health and disease, India was wrought with powerful, poignant, often painful contrasts. Even though I became very good friends with a number of Indians at the East-West Center, they were all highly educated (and almost certainly from the wealthier class), I would never have had the chance to have been exposed to a fundamental understanding of the breadth of Indian culture, good and bad, unless I had been personally exposed to real life circumstances.

ooooooooo

Where: From Delhi to the Southern tip of India

What I saw: I had six weeks to get to the southern tip of India and to end up in Colombo, Ceylon (now Sri Lanka) to catch a pre-booked ship back to Sydney in time for Christmas 1964. This part of the trip with a number of layovers in cities was all by third-class train to survive on my minimal budget.

The first leg was from Delhi to Jaipur, the "Pink City," so named because of the color of the buildings, including a striking and opulent colonnaded City Palace.

The next leg took me to Ahmadabad which I recall as more of a large industrial city. Given everything else I had already been exposed to in India, there was little that felt memorable.

I went onto Bombay (now Mumbai), the largest city of India. I was now much more in a mode as a tourist, as I had become far more comfortable—with regard to my emotional exposure—to the "shocking" aspects of India, its lifestyle, and its culture. It was great to see the ocean again and to be in an ocean port. I clearly remember the massive Gateway of India monument.

My next layover was Poona (now Pune) which was a couple of hours by train into the mountains. This was the retreat into the cooler mountains for the British colonists to get away from the oppressive heat and humidity of Bombay. It also became a retreat for some Maharajas and their families. It is also where Gandhi's ashes are buried in a garden. It is ironic that his final resting place should be so beautiful and peaceful compared to his existence as a martyr.

> "*I had become far more comfortable to the shocking aspects of India.*"

My next stop was Hyderabad which doesn't have any unique memories. Hyderabad in modern times has become a very influencing technology center of India and, in fact, in the world, but—by now—I was almost becoming blasé about life in India. I had found purpose and motivation and was ready to move toward it and offer change to the world in my manner as a private citizen.

My last major stopover before the train ride to the southern tip of India, was Madras (now Chennai). I was now a true tourist, spending my time visiting museums, going back to a British military fort from the seventeenth century and to the Headquarters of the East India Trading Company during the times of the British dominance of this part of the world. I thought back on India and the many people who didn't have a tourist's respite from their impoverishment.

> "*I thought back on India and the many people who didn't have a tourist's respite from their impoverishment.*"

As I had time at the main railway station waiting for my last train ride, I ordered a curried lamb meal. To this day, I remember this *Madras Meal* as the hottest thing I've ever consumed. Tears flowed out of my eyes, my face turned red, and my whole body was sweating. As I was almost out of money I couldn't afford to buy another meal, so it was this caloric fire or nothing.

What I thought: *It was red-faced, sweating, and crying that I would leave India . . . how fitting.*

ooooooooo

Some pictures of everyday Indian life would never leave my mind.

Images like these would help to shape my legacy for the rest of my life.

Where: The final leg – India to Ceylon and ship to Sydney

The next two days took me to the southern port where I caught a ferry boat to Ceylon (now Sri Lanka), but my departure from India was not over yet. This time, I had to exit through the Immigration office. I was held up. I did not have an entry stamp from crossing in the middle of the night back from Birgunj in Nepal to India. At that time, India may have been the most administratively bureaucratic country in the world. They ordered that I return to the nearest Immigration office in Madras to clear up my processing. This meant I was going to miss my ship trip out of Colombo. I knew enough about travel in India by now that I was able to produce a U.S. ten-dollar bill, and no further questions were asked. Alex Hamilton was crossing international borders for decades before anybody had heard of Lin Manuel Miranda.

After taking the ferry boat across to the northwest coast of Ceylon, I then took a train to Anuradhapura in north-central Ceylon, one of the most fascinating cities of my trip.

The city of Anuradhapura is one of the ancient capitols of Ceylon, has well preserved ruins of the ancient civilization, and is one of the oldest, continuously inhabited cities in the world. It is now a United Nations Educational, Scientific and Cultural Organization (UNESCO) World Heritage site. Of personal interest to me on this trip was that it was the center of Buddhism for many centuries. I continued on to Kandy in the mountains, a place that historically had been the early capital of the Sri Lankan kings. It is also the center for growing world famous Ceylon tea and for the Temple of the Tooth (a place of worship that houses the relic of the tooth of the Buddha).

I finally came to Colombo, the capitol of Ceylon where I would board the ship bound for Sydney.

What I thought: I had prepared for my trip to each country by reading books ahead of time about the cities on my trip and about national cultures and idiosyncrasies. *Both during and after the trip, I recognized that as much as preparation is important, it is real time and real events that are the final basis for success, for appreciating what happens in real life, and for adapting to the unexpected— both physically and emotionally—as one's circumstances dictate.*

A valuable preparatory advice I'd had before my trip was to carry U.S. and United Kingdom monies in a hidden money belt for safety. The tip allowed me to use the black market for currency conversion in India at a twelve times the official exchange rate. It also helped me to travel through India at a real cost of just fifty cents per day. Moreover, I was also able to buy antique religious collectables at a low cost with hard currencies and these collectibles have become priceless over time, not just in their monetary value, but also in the reminders they represent to me, reminders of the people, events, and emotions I experienced, reminders of the purpose I'd discovered, and reminders of who I had promised myself I'd become.

Where: After a life-changing journey of almost seven months, I travelled from Colombo and finally to Sydney by ship

After disciplined management of drinking and eating in conditions of poverty since leaving Honolulu, it was now time to relax, and eat and drink whatever I chose on a British ship. Not quite. Two days out of Colombo, I came down with dysentery as did half the passengers on the ship. The ship had taken on a tank of water in Aden that, when released into the ship's water supply, proved to be polluted. I wasn't the only one who found it ironic that I'd spent seven months in developing nations only to get ill on a British ship.

By the time I reached Sydney in mid-December 1964, I had fully recovered, but with vivid, in-tact memories and life influences that have been part of my daily existence ever since. Those memories have helped mold me into the person I am today.

ooooooooo

" . . . reminders of the people, events, and emotions I experienced, reminders of the purpose I'd discovered, and reminders of who I promised myself I'd become. "

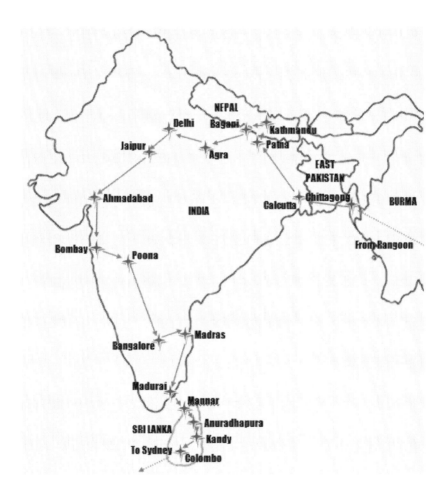

*With Japan Pop-
Out Map* ----->

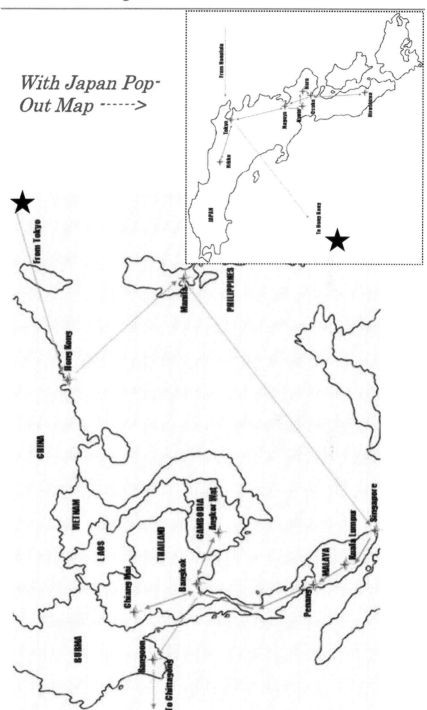

So You Can Define Your Purpose, Consider These Questions:

"Things turn out the best for the people who make the best of the way things turn out."

-John Wooden, basketball coach and author

1 – What is it that drives or motivates you in the life you want to live?

2 – When seeking to create change in your life, (*positive, forward movement*) what historical factors in your past should you consider?

3 – Take notes below about what specific professional or personal changes you are seeking now:

Iain Macfarlane

The Power of the

PRESENT-FUTURE Mindset

... So You Can Reach Where You're Going

"Mind is indeed the Builder . . . what is held in the act of mental vision becomes a reality in the material experience. We are gradually built to that image created within our own mental being."

~Edgar Cayce, American Mystic

*A*fter Christmas at home in Australia in 1964, I moved to Pittsburgh for my job at Heinz. My trip to Pittsburgh took me from Sydney with layovers in Singapore, Athens, Rome, and London.

When I had been in Calcutta on my post EWC Asian trip, I started to realize that – if I was going to make a difference going forward – it had to be on providing solutions that would be totally different from what I had originally anticipated. People choose their own ways of living. There are some that have a life forced on them, but they live it as they see fit. As an individual overwhelmed by the struggles of the developing world in which I'd been immersed, I didn't feel I could be impactful in a purely 'idealistic' way; commercially, however, I now thought I could make a difference. My focused education to understand these worlds taught me that I could bring commercialism to their world to make a difference economically (and therefore in so many other ways). Most of my journey, through to my first "grown-up" job with Heinz, had been done with a Past-Present Mindset. What happened to make things as they were?

Why were the Aborigines outcasts?

Why did I fear the curtains blowing in my childhood window?

Why did people believe differently?

Why was there drastic, economic development contrast in the world?

In India, something changed in me. How things became wasn't as important as how I could play a part in making them better for the future. My trip led to the PRESENT-FUTURE Mindset.

I'd spent much of my life as a risk-taker, as demonstrated through my experiences, and realized that it was an inherent element to my personality. While it's not a necessary trait for moving from a Past-Present Mindset to a PRESENT-FUTURE Mindset, I believe the characteristic did make it an easier transition for me. Risks often have to do with not knowing the outcome. The same is true for the PRESENT-FUTURE Mindset. This doesn't mean that I should be reckless; future-looking plans should include analysis of the past to make informed predictions and decisions. Nonetheless, there is the reality of uncertainty with most PRESENT-FUTURE Mindset applications.

Most of the Past-Present Mindset focus was about recognizing realities, rather than fixing or changing them to make a positive difference. With a new and powerfully motivated PRESENT-FUTURE Mindset, I started thinking about doing things I had not previously experienced and taking actions. I felt like I could do more in the food industry and commercial world, helping the commercial sector to expand what they were doing into the impoverished countries to make a bigger impact. With my previous 'philanthropy approach', things were being given without consequential purpose. It was easy to just send money toward hope for a change. With a plan, though, I could actually help to affect that change.

In order for commercial businesses to be successful, they are going to focus on areas where they can make a difference for consumers or else people won't buy their products; it's driven by a marketing thought and approach. My real life experiences led me back to my marketing training in college. I started to realize from a marketing perspective, I could identify a need and then provide a solution. After my EWC experiences and my Asia/India trip, I realized that I wanted to (and had the power to) create an opportunity for success and effect change in that way.

At this stage in my life, I had a belief that I came to through these experiences, but the reality still had to be proven. I needed to understand how to build a business to satisfy a need. By going into India, being exposed to the people and problems of the nation, and finding a solution to developing foods appropriate to their market that were commercially viable, a commercial company could have the opportunity to raise living standards. If others followed that direction over time, it would also potentially allow different markets to be developed in similar situations to India. A few years after I returned to Australia Heinz corporate did commercially open up operations in India and other developing nations.

Commerce doesn't have to be the enemy of culture. On the contrary, the two can be partners in positive improvement.

When I went out into the 'wide' world, first as a hitchhiker in New Zealand, then to the East-West Center including U.S. experiences, and later through my journey of exploration through India and Asia, I was thinking about going back and leaving the world for a while. I'd considered philosophizing, possibly in Thailand and the influence of Buddhism, based on my attraction to the issues of that part of the world.

I realized that thinking wasn't actually DOING_anything; it wasn't making actions occur!

I needed to change my activities and do things in a way which, with a commercial aspect to it, would result in the private sector putting resources to work to change the world for the better. My Past-Present Mindset didn't focus on what could be done differently. The solution could not be philanthropic alone . . . it needed to also be commercial.

I remember the nightmares that accompanied the curtains which blew into the window while I lay simultaneously fearful and sleepless in my childhood bed. I had created my own Past-Present Mindset. As an adult, it was time to exhale, send the curtains back out, and see the world through a PRESENT-FUTURE Mindset.

The winds of change were now in play.

ooooooo

I had acquired a conscious awareness of The Power of the PRESENT-FUTURE Mindset and it would be the most powerful driver of my future life... it would become the most important LIFE principle to measure my decision making skills and my positive results focused life.

"The winds of change were now in play. I had acquired a conscious awareness of The Power of the PRESENT-FUTURE Mindset."

"Commerce doesn't have

to be the enemy of culture."

~I.M.

The Power of People

. . . So You Can Experience Influence

The best way to find yourself is to lose yourself in the service of others.

~Mahatma Gandhi

"You can get everything in life you want if you will just help enough people to get what they want."

~Zig Zigler, Author and
Motivational Speaker

A ccording to Dictionary.com, an "epiphany" is a sudden, intuitive perception of, or insight into, the reality or essential meaning of something, usually initiated by some simple, homely, or commonplace occurrence or experience. While I couldn't look back on my cultural and travel experiences, prior to entering the workforce, as commonplace, I could look at them with new eyes – with the eyes of my epiphany to face the world with a PRESENT-FUTURE Mindset. That future-looking change allowed me to look *back* and discover even more lessons than I had realized I'd experienced without being a constraint or comfort zone emotion in my decision making.

In my life, I had many people who had affected influence in my own life. They were the ones who I wished to emulate to affect change in the lives of others and in my world.

Educational Influencers

Anyone that attended Barker College during **William Leslie**'s headmastership, was known as one of "Leslie's Men." He was considered one of the best headmasters in Australia, not because of technical skill but because of relationship and leadership skills.

I was turning sixteen in my final year of high school at Barker. Early in that school year, Headmaster Leslie had privately told my parents that he wanted me to come back for an extra year to repeat the final year of high school. He recognized that I had good leadership skills and he wanted to work with me for another year. At the end of the year, I'd already taken my final exams in November with the results to come out in January. My parents asked me to go along with them to see the Headmaster. He told me he expected that I would have passed my final exams and would have qualified to move onto university. He then told me what it would mean to me to have another full year in school; he described what it would mean in my life to have the opportunity to be a leader. I was able to see a different vision, which is not an easy story to tell a sixteen-year-old who is ready to go into the world. I didn't realize at the time he was using a PRESENT-FUTURE Mindset on me!

When I went back for that extra year, I took additional honors courses (economics and geography), was elected a

Prefect, became a Company Commander in ROTC, played sports as a part of the football, cricket, and golf School teams, and was even in a school play. These experiences would have been lost without that additional year. Also, I had to grow up as a Prefect. I learned:

- o Leadership
- o Accountability
- o Academic Influence

I ended up with a Commonwealth Scholarship and an Australian Steel Industry Scholarship to pay my full way to at Sydney University. I had qualified a year earlier; now I qualified with many more experiences to prepare me for my next stage in life –university education and experiences.

In my last year at Barker College, I had the great honor and responsibility of being one of the pall bearers when Mr. Leslie passed away.

ooooooooo

I was lucky to be influenced by a number of great educators, in addition to William Leslie. **Trevor McCaskill** was, for two years, my English Teacher. He brought English alive by making us role model, perform. He personally was an active participant in whatever we were dealing with.

He gave me the love of Shakespeare.

He taught me to be insightful in learning.

He even had to take on sex education in the school, so he saw all of us at our most vulnerable while we learned about the things we didn't want to ask about.

McCaskill also was my rugby football coach in my second year of High School. He came down to football practice after class and got down there, running with us and working alongside us. To see somebody who was my *teacher*, coming down and playing *on level terms* with us, made me realize that we were more than a job for him . . . he cared about us as people! About twenty years later, McCaskill returned from teaching at other high schools as the Headmaster of Barker College.

ooooooooo

In my extra year of school, **Mr. Farr** taught me economics . . . and sports! I worked with him on honors economics to learn lifelong professional skills. Then, he worked with me one-on-one and as a part of the team for cricket. Farr showed real interest in my education and went out of his way to engage me on every level of personal development, both in-school and after-school hours.

ooooooooo

Reverend Hugh Dixon was the School Chaplain with one class a week for each Grade. He was a very spiritual versus evangelical leader. He wanted us to learn the life lessons that came from scriptures. You could talk to him about anything. His influence on me strengthened my resolve to respect individuals no matter who they were.

He was also a Captain in the Australian Army and he was a leader in our ROTC training. He was always a calming influence when we were in field training in tough military environments.

He was the person any one of us at school could talk to about issues of life.

Sports Influencers

In my teenage years, at Barker College, my closest friends were the result of shared passion for sports. At holidays, we would play cricket in the backyards. Of my four closest friends, three played representative team cricket later in life. As families, we would also go as a group with one of the parents at the beach to take in a game, as well as go surfing. We were ALWAYS competing. That competition instilled a desire to be successful for the win. We also played tennis and competed. In the summer, we swam in our neighbor's pool and kept records. My close, personal friendships with **John, Doug, and Phil Blazey**, as well as **with Neil and Lynn Marks**, allowed me to be extremely competitive in nature – they were all top level sports performers.

oooooooo

At Sydney University, I continued my close friendship with the Blazey brothers and developed another close and lifelong friendship with **David Clark**, who went to a rival school. He was an outstanding athlete in cricket and rugby. David and I won the Foursomes Golf championship (which has only two people per team) while at Sydney University. When I was at Heinz in Pittsburgh, David was getting his MBA degree at Harvard Business School and we met up a few times (including his wife) during that period. The lesson I learned with David Clark was the value of competition while always looking ahead at the value of long term close relationships. We would be friends for decades across the continents that kept our professional lives busy, until he succumbed to cancer later in life.

Even after I moved permanently to the U.S. we kept in touch as he started in Sydney a Merchant Bank that he eventually grew into the fourth largest in the world (Macquarie Bank). He also talked me into becoming a Founder Member of Tennessee National Golf Club near Knoxville, Tennessee, as he was the primary funder of the great Australian golfer,

> "*There is such a thing as mutual benefit, even when somebody's public status is greater.*"

Greg Norman, who designed and built the course. In his other life, David had become Chairman of the Australian Rugby Union and Chairman of the Australian Opera.

I learned to surround myself with other successful people, rather than to be intimidated by them. Share and learn from those who have successful career paths of their own. There is value in learning from other successful people. It has often been called the Law of Attraction.

oooooooo

Through a lifelong comfort level with sports figures, I gained the confidence to be able to approach people who have celebrity status. There *is* such a thing as MUTUAL benefit, even when somebody's public status is greater. My lack of intimidation and my self-confidence in this area led to an ability to approach people to discover mutual benefit throughout my professional career.

When returning to Australia with Heinz in Melbourne in January of 1967, I looked for products in the U.S. that would be suitable for the Australian market. One product newly successful in the U.S. was Gatorade, which had been launched before my return to Australia and it proved highly successful in the sporting world. I thought a good spokesperson in Australia for the product would be Ron Clarke; I knew he would be effective.

In 1956, when the Olympics were in Melbourne, and even though Ron was a teenage prodigy as a runner, he still could not make the Australian team because of the country's status at the time of being the leading country in the world for middle distance runners. Nonetheless, as a tribute to his ability, Ron Clarke was secretly selected for the honor to be the final runner into the stadium with the torch to light the Olympic Flame. His *arm* was burnt with dripping oil as he held the torch high for ten seconds before lighting the Olympic Flame at the top of the stadium; he never flinched. He allowed focus, intensity, and strength to take over. He had a lifetime scar.

Ron Clarke was the world's leading middle distance runner at the time that I returned to Australia in 1967 from Heinz in Pittsburgh and during his career he held seventeen world records. I approached Ron about the concept of the new product like Gatorade. He was well aware of Gatorade. He agreed that he'd like to be part of the development and to be a sponsor of an equivalent product to Gatorade. A development team at Heinz back-engineered Gatorade to recreate a comparable product that could generate similar benefits for athletes. Ron was the first sponsor. He worked with me very closely on positioning and promoting in the Australian marketplace and we were successful with "Vigorade." There could not have been a better sponsor.

Because Ron and I were identical in size, and Ron was always being given athletic attire by those who wanted his sponsorship or wanted him to test their product, he would routinely pass new things onto me. In 1967, he was a tester of a new shoe that would become one such hand-me-down. That's how I got to run in the original Nike shoes, before the company was even named Nike!

Because of my personal relationship with Ron, I was asked by TV Channel 7 in Sydney to get (maybe even 'con') Ron to Sydney without his knowing that he was going to be the recipient of the Show, "This is Your Life... Ron Clarke". With the help of my wife, we got him to the Channel 7 studio without his realizing he was to be the feature. (We also had to get his wife, Helen, up from Melbourne and into the audience without Ron knowing).

I stayed friends with Ron for years. He was always intense and successful. Breaking records. Winning. It carried on after running when he became Lord Mayor of the fourth largest mayoral district in Australia, the Gold Coast of Queensland. He held that position for many years until he chose to retire. Ron was one of many people I knew who were successful because of being able to carry their athletic intensity into the business world and my relationship with Ron only increased my confidence in approaching leaders to do what they do best . . . LEAD.

ooooooooo

In the case of Vigorade, consecutively, I signed **Geoff Hunt** (a seven-time world championship Squash winner) as a sponsor, and later, **Jonah Barrington** (a Welshman who was a four-time world champion Squash winner). Personally, I had the opportunity to play against each of them in friendly Squash games, bringing back my own Squash skills from my days as captain of the Sydney University team. I of course didn't beat them, but I did get to play them! It was as inVIGORADEing as playing golf games later in life in the U.S. with **Hubie Greene, David Graham, Hale Irwin** and **Greg Norman,** all winners of golf Majors.

ooooooooo

So often people are given opportunities to do something with the GREATS of that "thing" and they balk at the chance because they aren't equally gifted in that area. We need to be competent, but I don't have to be perfect. We certainly don't have to be afraid of such rare chances in our lifetimes. We should have respect for the opportunities afforded us.

Sports continued to play a huge part in my success in my career as a marketing and business professional. As with my educational influencers, recognizing lessons from my relationships dating back to my schoolboy years and extending into my career, made it more clear to me that life lessons gained from experiences and connections could lead to lifetime relationships by choice.

Professional Influencers

When I was at Columbia University in New York in the first semester of the second year of my MBA program (September 1963-February 1964), a number of business recruiters from major corporations came to interview graduating students. I had a lot of serious conversations of interest with Ford, Procter & Gamble, and McKinsey Management Consultants. I wanted to find a company that could give me two years in the U.S., and then send me back to their Australian operation. I had considered Procter & Gamble, but the closest they could get me to home was Hong Kong as they did not operate in Australia at that time. Ford had operations in Australia but couldn't guarantee I'd be sent back there. Management in McKinsey liked me and arranged for me to spend a day with **Rod Carnegie**. He'd formed McKinsey in Australia a couple of years earlier and, prior to that, he had been a star in their New York office. I was only twenty-three at the time and Rod explained to me that he thought I could do a fabulous job. However, to be a respected management consultant in Australia at this time where the old-school model of working from the bottom up to be in executive leadership, I would need to get four to five years of real world operating experience before becoming a management consultant.

At the end of the meeting he did get my attention; he had an ideal potential opportunity for me at that time. McKinsey had just re-organized the marketing and sales structure for Heinz in Pittsburgh. Heinz was rebuilding their whole Marketing

Division. Rod connected me with Heinz Pittsburgh. Would I be interested in an interview? (YES!) They were recruiting fourteen people for marketing. I was offered a position that included the opportunity to go back to Australia after two years. I started in January of 1965, following my Asia/India tour.

What I really appreciated from spending the day with Rod was his honesty in setting me on a path that turned out to be as good as I could have ever considered. In fact, he took me from a Past-Present Mindset to a PRESENT-FUTURE Mindset where I could visualize being a successful Management Consultant a few years in the future.

oooooooo

Burt Gookin was recruited by Heinz in 1964 to be the new CEO to lead the turnaround of the Heinz Company. He had gone through Northwestern on a boxing scholarship and we had a connection because I had also been a boxer at Barker College. Burt knew I was going to be heading back to Australia in two years as part of my deal with Heinz. He reached out to me to make me feel at home while in Pittsburgh. I had meals with he and his wife at their home and he gave me a sense of relationship in the corporate world.

I had an opportunity to work with Burt at his invitation in 1966 on a project when he was the Chairman of the Grocery Manufacturers Association (GMA). He had an idea. Would I be willing to help him fill it out? (Again, YES!) The simplicity of his idea was that if you could put scanning symbols on the product and scanned it at checkout in supermarkets, the database of the inventory would adjust when somebody checked out. When inventory dropped to a minimum level for the store, it would automatically reorder from a central warehouse. Again, at a minimum level in the central supermarket warehouse the computerized system would automatically order from the manufacturer. The idea of UPC scanning back in 1966 is now in practice across the entire commercial world, today.

ooooooooo

My Heinz influencers went straight to the heart of the company. **John Heinz III** had previously finished his Harvard MBA and had now decided to join Heinz; he did so one week after me and we ended up with adjoining offices in the Marketing Department. He was two years older than me and we worked on some projects together. And both, as bachelors at the time, spent a number of late nights together (partying). When I had my Buck's party (bachelor's party for my non-Aussies), he organized it for me. A few years later he left Heinz and became a Congressman, then Senator for Pennsylvania, highly respected by both sides of the aisle. He was a centrist amongst Republicans and just slightly right of Democrats. He shared with many that he was intending to run for President in 2000 when he would have been sixty-two; unfortunately, he was killed in 1992 in a small plane when he had a mid-air collision with a helicopter. From John, I learned that you could pull things together from both sides of an issue personally, professionally, and even politically.

Personal Influencers

Malcolm Douglas was truly the *original* crocodile hunter.

I first met Malcolm Douglas in 1967 following his marriage to Val (King) who had been a close friend of mine in my post high school days. Malcolm's credibility, in reality, goes back a bit before the star of "*CRIKEY* Steve Irwin" to *Crocodile Dundee*, whose hunting exploits were based on Malcolm Douglas's own experiences and knowledge of crocodiles. In addition, Douglas had been a mentor to Steve Irwin until Steve was tragically killed by a stingray in the much-covered rare, freak accident during which the stinger pierced Irwin's heart while out at sea.

Pictured below, Val and Malcolm Douglas stand outside their Australian home on the crocodile farm in Broome, Western Australia.

Malcolm and I were connected in an Aussie style based on our own forms of intensity and as risk takers (although his risks were more life threatening than most of my exploits – although that's probably for another story).

Malcolm had lived with Aboriginal tribes and created fifty film documentaries of the

The crocodiles of Malcolm's "farm" including: a full-grown adult, a "baby's nest," and Iain holding a young crocodile.

Outback and recorded rare footage of some sacred rituals of the Aborigines (the only white person known to have been allowed to film this ceremony). He was recognized as an icon of Australia as a true explorer, even discovering some native animals for the first time. While living in Melbourne after I returned in 1967 from the U.S., Malcolm and my family had quite a bit of contact. Malcolm and Val asked me to read a proof of his first book, *"Across the Top"*, as well as reviewing his first documentary by the same name before its initial release on a rainy night in a tent on the Mornington Peninsula.

I last saw Malcolm and Val in 1998, on his massive crocodile farm in Broome, Western Australia. Before we could see one another again, while working on his farm one night in the truck he used for his work (a big Land Rover with remote controls to navigate the rough terrain), Malcolm ended up tragically getting hit by his own vehicle and pinned against a tree. A true Australian hero was lost, but not before he reminded me of my Outback roots and helped me to share them with my own children.

Through the interactions with Malcolm, Val and also her parents in the Outback where we stayed on vacations, I hope I have been able to instill some of that *openness, wanderlust, ruggedness, and warrior spirit* of a breed of Aussies. And these Outback experiences gave examples to my family of dealing with the unknown situations in the rugged Outback lifestyle in a PRESENT-FUTURE Mindset, being prepared for anything, that could never have been achieved with a comfort level mindset.

ooooooooo

A personal influence related to "the world of power" led me unknowingly (at the time) to one of four contacts over a period of twenty years related to the CIA. This influence first came from my friendship with **Sir Phillip Lynch** that started when we met as parents of similar aged children in Mt. Eliza after Madge and I moved to Australia in 1967.

He had been elected to the Australian Federal Parliament just before we met and the first critical experience in his political career came in 1968 when he was Minister for the Army and the My Lai massacre in Vietnam involving U.S. Servicemen went public. As the father of a U.S. Marine, I recognize that a majority of servicemen and women are honorable people of the uniform who value human life and experiences, but My Lai was a dark mark. Lynch was immediately asked by the Australian media whether any Australian Servicemen might have been involved in that or similar incidents. He responded in live interviews with, "There is not a scintilla of evidence that Australians were involved". Blank stares from the media. His immediate lesson was to only use laymen terms when communicating with the media who themselves communicate in layman terms. Phillip later became Deputy Leader of the Liberal Party (actually, the conservative party in Australia!) from 1972-1982.

After I moved to Sydney in 1972 to join the advertising agency, SPASM, my next contact came from Phillip in 1974 to see if my agency would be interested in handling the advertising for the Federal elections. We said yes, particularly as we personally were opposed to the radical Labour Party policies since they had been elected to power in 1972. I was approached by **Frank Nugan**, the younger brother of my roommate through Sydney University, to say he had a number of clients from the bank he owned in the Cayman Islands who wanted to financially support our advertising campaign. He became the largest donor to the whole campaign. Although the Labour Party won the election the Prime Minister, Gough Whitlam, was removed by the Governor-General (this has been considered the greatest political and constitutional crisis in Australian history) and another election was held in 1975 that brought the Liberal Party overwhelmingly back into power by the largest margin in history.

Frank's bank, the Nugan-Hand Bank in the Cayman Islands was actually a front for the CIA (it turned out **Michael Hand**, his partner in the Bank, was a CIA Agent) who often used financial funds rumored to have been generated by drug dealings in the 'Golden Triangle' of Thailand, Burma and Laos. The U.S. Government had been voicing its objections to the Whitlam foreign policy implemented when Whitlam came to power in 1972 to keep U.S. military out of Australia including banning any U.S. Navy ships from calling into Australian ports.

The Nugan-Hand Bank collapsed and Frank Nugan was found dead in his Mercedes in a small country town from 'self inflicted' gunshot wounds. After exhuming his body a few years later, it was proven he must have been murdered. This whole story is documented in a book published in 1987 by New York Times investigative reporter, Jonathan Kwitney titled, "The Crimes of Patriots".

My first involvement with the CIA actually had occurred in 1964 when I was at the East-West Center. Some rumors had been spread that the EWC that had been initiated by Lyndon Johnson in 1960 was actually an undercover operating front for the CIA to both recruit bright young foreign candidates as well as being an opportunity for U.S. CIA members, as students at the EWC, to travel under cover to Asia and Pacific countries as part of the exchange program at the EWC requiring them to spend one to two semesters in Asia or Pacific countries.

In March 1964, an Assistant Secretary of State visited the EWC to put together an investigative Committee to hold public hearings on this potential political situation. An American EWC student was asked to be Chairman of the Committee, I was asked to be Vice Chairman and the other members were an EWC Administrator, two University of Hawaii students and two Hawaii business people. We held a number of public meetings over two weeks. Our conclusion published two weeks later was we did not find any evidence to support the rumor. Post reflection: the American Chairman, it turned out, was also employed—while at the EWC—by the Rand Corporation and spent a few years working in Asia post EWC. Maybe a connection?

My third "contact" with the CIA occurred in 1986 when I was living in New York City and took on a consulting job, on the side, to an Australian who had formed a company in New York and who wanted my business guidance on how to grow his business. Over a number of years he had created a software package to allow the translation of English written content into French and vice versa. His first client had been the Canadian Government and then he added some companies in the private sector. He had also added German and Russian languages for bi-language translation.

After two months of working with him I was reviewing the process of how he had gained the Soviet Government as a client. A person had walked in "off the street" and he had signed an agreement to translate various product/machine operating manuals that they would give him to be translated from English into Russian. It was a lucrative business. On further discussion, I discovered the CIA had also contacted him and were giving him directions on putting incorrectly "translated" directions in certain elements of the operating instructions (to frustrate the Soviets using the translated instructions!). I resigned my consulting agreement that day!!!

My fourth "contact" occurred around September 1992 when my son Jeff was approached by the CIA. He was in his Junior Year at East Tennessee State University in the undergraduate business program. The CIA had a one year college program where they took a number of students to work at CIA Headquarters in Langley, Virginia, between their Junior and Senior years and then they return to their college to complete their Senior year. Jeff went through a detailed process of providing information, meeting with a field officer, and our neighbors (and probably others) were interviewed. Jeff was selected to go to a five day final evaluation and selection process in December 1992 in the CIA testing center in McLean, Virginia.

In McLean, Jeff signed a document that he would never in his life reveal what went on during his five days at the CIA. The same is required of other servicemen and women, as well as civilian agents who go through similar training and events. To this day, all Jeff has revealed is that he never wants to go through that experience ever again. Jeff was selected to go to the CIA in Langley in June 1993. In February 1993 he received a FedEx package telling him the offer had been withdrawn as the newly elected Democrat President, President Bill Clinton, had put a freeze on new hiring for the CIA and FBI. Jeff did join the U.S. Marine Corps after completing his senior year and has since retired from the USMC after twenty years of service, ultimately earning the rank of Lieutenant Colonel.

ooooooooo

We live the lives we lead because of the connections we have amongst family, friends, colleagues, and even random brushes with "secret agents". If we always look to connect the people in our lives to the experiences in our lives, to the lessons we can learn from those experiences, there is value in every relationship we make and maintain. I'm grateful for personal, professional, athletic, and government connections as they have helped to shape me as an individual.

What people in your life:

- o *Help to define your values?*
- o *Grow you as an individual?*
- o *Affirm your principles and drivers?*

The Power of Entrepreneurship

. . . So You Can Affect Influence

"To do a common thing uncommonly well brings success."

~Henry J. Heinz, Founder of Heinz Company

"The quality of a person's life is in direct proportion to their commitment to excellence, regardless of their field of endeavor."

~Vince Lombardi, American Football Player,
Coach Extraordinaire, Executive, and Motivator

I n 1974, I had then moved on from Heinz in Melbourne and was now working in Sydney as a partner of the advertising agency, SPASM who I had joined in 1972. Unfortunately for anyone in advertising in 1974, all were suffering through the serious collapse of the Australian (and global) economy.

What do you do when you come up against a brick wall?

1. Stop bashing your head against the wall.
2. Vow not to give up.
3. Step Back.
4. Look at the situation from a strategic perspective.
5. Be willing to take the risk of doing something different than traditional thinking or what you have been doing in the past.
6. Execute.

At this time much of our advertising client base was built on my personal background and experiences with Heinz in package goods marketing. My experience was appropriate for other blue-chip packaged goods clients who tended to be larger and committed advertisers. When interest rates soared to twenty seven percent during this economic downturn, those clients *immediately* cut their advertising budgets, as their advertising was longer, term based advertising rather than short term product/retail advertising. Cutting advertising was an immediate cash savings.

My partners and I talked for two days off-site to discuss how we should strategize through this. (Interestingly, I still prefer to work off-site with clients when working through vision and strategies as you can see the picture better from outside of it!)

"Who has a NEED to advertise in the economy with high interest rates?" we asked ourselves. Retailers needed to continue to spend in order to create traffic in their stores. They *had* to move product because of the interest costs on inventory.

We changed from a primary base of client marketing of packaged goods (branded consumables) advertising to retail advertising. However, we recognized that the best form of impact and reach advertising in the Sydney market (where we were operating) was television advertising. At this time, retailers rarely used TV and were primarily investing in print and radio ads. We now had a problem. In tough times like this, retailers are going to consider television excessively expensive . . . it was already higher cost than print advertising and radio to build a campaign. Head? Meet wall!!!

At that same time, a fourth major TV channel had recently launched in Sydney: Channel 10 (TEN). We approached them knowing they were struggling to sell time. We made a proposal to them that if we brought a retailer to them who had never advertised on television before, would they give us fifty percent rates for the first six months. They were also new entrepreneurs, so they immediately agreed.

We picked up department stores, auto dealers, supermarkets, fast food restaurants, and . . . WE. BUILT. OUR. BUSINESS. We became the fastest growing ad agency in Australia at the time with retailer focused advertising when other ad agencies continued to struggle. (AND businesses AND consumers, alike.) Because our client base was retailers, we learned to test and measure the results to demonstrate the effectiveness of the television advertising. We were able to correlate, every week and sometimes daily, what was happening between their store sales and the products we had featured. At the same time as this approach was a breakthrough medium of advertising for this retailer base, we needed Channel 10 to agree to allow us to immediately change our commercials at basically any time if the commercials were not working. We had an agreement to change commercials weekly. We also, for the first time, got the channel to allow us to use their studios for production to accommodate that rapid change and at a much lower cost than the traditional cost of producing commercials (for our *cost- sensitive* retailers). We also had to create a new WEEKLY billing system. It was an operational issue. (Operational adjustments may be necessary as a result of strategic planning.)

As with the mutual benefit I had learned through sporting sponsorships between popular athletes and consumer products, Channel 10 grew significantly by partnership of our ad agency with retail marketers; this relationship was a breakthrough in comparison to the other traditional Channels. Channel 10 was looked at by the other, slow-to-change channels, as being disruptive to doing business the way they had always done it. (When was the last time the world took notice of somebody for doing something as it had always been done before?) This was a successful strategic partnership...it was coopetition.

> "*When was the last time the world took notice of somebody for doing something as it had always been done before?*"

When I joined the workforce with Heinz in the U.S., following my East-West Center experiences, it was with the purpose of using commercial means to affect positive cultural change and success. In the midst of an economic crisis, I was seeing that happen. A new business (Channel 10) was flourishing; long-standing businesses (retailers) were seeing sales increase despite seemingly insurmountable interest rates; and forward movement was occurring in my own company. Businesses were successful; jobs were saved; paychecks put food on tables; and children were growing up resilient in my native Australia.

oooooooo

The first Australian Pizza Hut opened in Belfield, Sydney in April, 1970, but the chain had not yet made its mark on the culture. In its efforts to succeed in Australia particularly in an economic downturn, Pizza Hut founder in the U.S., Frank Carney, came knocking on the door of SPASM. Seeing the success we were having in the Australian retailer market, he discussed how we could take their product and make it successful in Australia. My worlds were colliding. I had extensive knowledge in the consumables market and now well-developed processes for retail advertising and marketing to Australians. I needed to bring in some additional lessons, though. I thought back to the cultural lessons of my East-West Center days. That's where I learned that you couldn't simply translate things linguistically; you must also do so culturally; I knew the same would surely hold true for marketing. The popular toppings and offerings from the U.S. were not all going to "translate" to Australian tastes.

We decided to try something new and draw upon my prior experiences at Heinz in Melbourne: *focus groups*. At that time, bringing consumers into the conversation *before* as part of the product development process, as well creating sales and marketing ideas for promotional plans, was not a common practice. We had earned a reputation that afforded us the flexibility to try something new. There were discussions and taste tests to determine the "flavors" that would work well in Australia. After much deliberation with these focus groups, a truly unique new pizza was created; it was a traditional pizza of red sauce and mozzarella on a crust, but its toppings would be . . . *ham and pineapple!* Today, the "Hawaiian Pizza," is the most popular international choice and some version of it is featured with virtually every major pizza chain – originally developed by us in Sydney, Australia!!!

In total, we created six unique Australian flavors and this resulted in a major business success for Pizza Hut in Australia.

oooooooo

If marketing could play a role in national economic recovery, and global business success, there had to be a way to use it to bring some of my own passions to a greater audience (to accommodate even more positive change in the world).

Cricket had been a passion to me from as far back as I could remember. I first began playing competitively in fourth grade at Pennant Hills Public School. We had our own cricket field at the school and Sydney's long Spring, Summer, Autumn and mild Winter seasons were always conducive to playing outdoors. At the time I was growing up, cricket was the most popular sport in the country and international matches received extensive coverage in the press and on the radio (as black and white TV did not become available in Australia until I was finishing High School and color TV was many years later; we learned to listen very well!). Australians, young and old, were active participants in sports as a genetic way of life and we were always very competitive.

I was a good cricket player for many years and was often elected captain of the teams for which I played. From grade school through high school at Barker College, and then four years for the University of Sydney, where in 1960-1961 I achieved the then record for most wickets bowling in a season; cricket was a part of my life.

As with all adults, life came calling and the sport and I had a break while I was at the East-West Center, when I was working in Pittsburgh with Heinz, and — of course — when my focus was on getting married and returning to Australia with my young family. After one year back in Australia, I knew the passion had never left me and I joined a district team in Melbourne. We won the premiership in two of the three years I got to play (I won the MVP Medal in both Final matches) before my family; then we moved to Sydney in May 1972.

In Sydney I joined Waverley District Cricket Club, one of the oldest and historically most successful clubs in Sydney. I also became a member of the Board of Directors. This area of Sydney was showing a significant reduction of the younger generation and the available young cricket talent was also declining. The Club had not won the Sydney championship in more than thirty years.

As a person who liked to win, after the 1974-1975 season, I made a unique proposal to the Board. Our summer was the English winter and top cricket players in England had to find other jobs. Cricket was not a full time profession in any part of the world. I proposed we find a top cricket talent in England with charisma and promotional skills and bring that person to

Sydney to play for Waverley, holding coaching clinics for kids and promote the game in our district with public relations opportunities. I also said I would package an offer to contract the player for our 1975-1976 Summer season.

The player we selected, and the one I called, was Tony Greig. At that time he was Captain of the England team and one of the dominant players in cricket globally. After taking my cold call he asked me to call him again a few days later to give him time to think about this opportunity. His compensation then was 10,000 UK pounds from cricket, his house mortgage, a new Jaguar car each year and some minor promotional money (a total value of approximately $30,000 U.S.).

With Kerry Packer (he was a media baron who became the wealthiest person in Australia) as a client, I was able to get him to be the major sponsor with $50,000AU, airfares for Tony's family and the cost of a rental home. Tony's obligation was to provide a weekly cricket article for the Daily Telegraph newspaper, an exclusive family interview to the largest magazine in Australia, the *Australian Women's Weekly*; broadcast on TV Channel 9 first class cricket games that did not conflict with his playing obligations for Waverley District Cricket Club; and—as a value-added gift to his sponsor— provide private cricket coaching to Kerry's son, James. The other two equal cash sponsors were Kellog's (the Marketing Director was a friend of mine) and Sears-Walton (I went to Barker College with the CEO, John Walton). Tony's obligations to these sponsors were TV commercials and store appearances. This compensation package had a value of $140,000 - $150,000 (U.S. equivalent).

We won the Sydney Championship for the first time in thirty-three years! Goal setting, thinking outside the box, a willingness to connect people in an innovative way, taking a risk, hard work and a continuing focus on the end result led to that win. However, what was born of a competitive Aussie nature, grew into so much more. As it turned out, this would be just the beginning of a major change to cricket globally, making the game the commercial and professional industry it has evolved into today.

oooooooo

As the late, great Paul Harvey would say, now here's the rest of the story . . .

Tony and his family returned to England in February 1976 for the summer cricket season in the Northern Hemisphere. As much as he wanted to come back to Australia for the next summer, he was unable to do so because he was committed to a cricket tour at the same time as the Captain of the England team. They were to tour the West Indies. Tony introduced me to another great England player who was not selected for the tour of the West Indies, Geoff Boycott. Geoff Boycott played for the Waverley team for the 1976-1977 season.

In mid-winter 1976, Kerry Packer came to my office to have a discussion about an issue he had been wrestling with for a couple of years. For a number years he had been broadcasting first class cricket in Australia on Channel 9, a company he owned, but he was unable get broadcast rights for international cricket between countries, particularly between Australia and England; the rights were controlled by each country's cricket control board who typically defaulted to government broadcasting stations. He even offered up to ten times what the government stations would pay and was still rejected by the two cricket control boards.

Problem: How to devise international cricket matches where he could own the broadcast rights. (Head? Meet wall!)

Solution: The concept we discussed was to contract the thirty best cricketers in the world from multiple nationalities into two groups of fifteen to play a series of five one-day games during the interim weather season between the Northern and Southern Hemispheres. We chose that timing so as not to conflict with the primary seasons in either hemisphere. (It took about three hours to come to that idea – an inordinate amount of time for Kerry!) Each player would be paid $25,000 (AU) for participating for four weeks, and then each would compete for $100,000 (winner take all) to be divided among the fifteen winning team members. Kerry would own the TV rights that he could use in the many playing countries of the world. He worked with John Cornell to develop the details of the program, including contacting some of the targeted Australian players who John Cornell represented as an agent to sound them out on the concept.

oooooooo

Tony Greig's next trip to Australia was in March 1977 to Captain the England team against Australia in the Centenary of the first cricket test that had been played in Melbourne in 1877. He invited me to be his guest at that March 12th to 17th, 1977 match. Before going to Melbourne, Kerry asked me to approach Tony about his interest in playing in his new cricket venture and he was probably a critical participant to make the concept work. I did not mention anything to Tony until the game ended as I did not want any possibility of conflict of interest for him due what we knew would be controversial for the cricket national controlling boards.

Tony agreed to meet with Kerry and he came back to Sydney and stayed at my home during these first few discussions. Tony also agreed to approach the targeted players on the England, South African, West Indies, and Pakistani teams. While I was not involved in the final discussions due to an extended business trip to the U.S. followed by my work with Doyle Dane Bernbach (DDB) from January 1978 in New York City, I was proud to be a part of what became *World Series Cricket*. The new endeavor launched in Australia toward the end of 1977. *World Series Cricket* drastically changed the global nature of the way cricket is played today, as well as creating an industry of full time professional players with cricket broadcast all over the world and some players making over a million dollars every year.

> "*World Series Cricket drastically changed the global nature of the way cricket is played today.*"

In addition, after his retirement, Tony became one of the most revered global cricket commentators ever. Tony remained one of my closest friends with visits to the U.S. and my own visits back to Australia until he passed away in 2012.

Tony Greig and Iain with the World Series Cricket Cup in 2006.

ooooooo

I had Power Influencers to affect so many aspects of my life. Now, it was time to grasp onto power to affect influence in (and for) others.

Iain's son, Rob, aged eight, bowling to Tony Greig, Captain of England, at Tony's home in Hove!

Iain was gifted a rare cricket bail from the 1977 match. This was one of only four bails used in the Centenary Match. A "priceless" gift!

"When I joined the work force, it was with the purpose of using commercial means to affect positive cultural change and success."

~I.M.

The Power of Knowing Yourself

. . . So You Can Use Your Power

"Formulate and stamp indelibly on your mind a mental picture of yourself as succeeding. Hold this picture tenaciously and never permit it to fade. Your mind will seek to develop this picture!

~Dr. Norman Vincent Peale

"An unexamined life is not worth living."

~Socrates, Philosopher and Writer

With my Australian nature revitalized, and hopefully—to a certain degree—understood and instilled in my family, a new chapter was about to begin. DDB sponsored my family's return to the U.S. through a six-year stint in global advertising. While in New York, I was eventually recruited by Venture Capitalists for the company, Power.Base Systems. Though it's not rare today, Power.Base was ahead of itself in requiring psychological exams of its recruits, not to determine their balance, so to speak, but rather to understand their personalities and how they would fit into a corporate culture. My own assessment would serve as another defining moment for me.

The exam, with an industrial psychology firm in New York, took place from 9:00 A.M. to 4:00 P.M. I got a lunch break and then there was an hour to review the insights that the psychologist had garnered from an analysis of *everything*.

When 4:00 arrived, the psychologist told me, "this will take five minutes."

He then proceeded to share that there were exactly two words that described me:

- o   CONCEPTUAL
- o   ADVOCATE

I have a strong, strategic, conceptual reading of situations and a need to be the advocate to make the plan for that concept to happen. In other words, for me, thinking is inherent, but doing is desired. I used those two words to lead me through more than twenty years of business successes before working as a coach.

As you move into the tools to build your own legacy, ask yourself, *'who am I?'* What words would describe you? What is inherent to your nature and personality and what is your desire? Reflect on your own life experiences including:

- o   Relationships
- o   Defining (epiphany) Moments
- o   Personal Drivers
- o   Professional Principles
- o   Recognized Influence from Others
- o   Past Applications of Influence

In these things is your power . . . *The Power of I Am . . . So I Can.* That is the power you will need to tap into in order to use the tools necessary to creating your own life legacy.

> **"As you move into the tools to build your own legacy, ask yourself, 'Who am I?'"**

"Reflect on yourself

and on your own experiences."

~I.M.

Part 3
Tools to Build
a Legacy

"Business, executive, and leadership coaching continues in an experiential and relational manner to Influence and Inspire business owners and leaders to come up with solutions, themselves."

~I.M.

The Power of the "IBGP"

. . . So You Can Work Toward Your Purpose

"In order to carry a positive action, we must develop here a positive vision."

~Dalai Lama

"The more organizations and people who learn to start with WHY, the more people there will be who wake up feeling fulfilled by the work they do."

-Simon Sinek, Author and Speaker

*I*n December of 2003, I was reflecting on my life balance between work and time spent with my son Rob, his wife Candy, and their son Jack. Rob had accepted a position that past July to do his four-year residency in anesthesiology at the University of Wisconsin Hospital. In that first six months of my son living nearby, I was commuting weekly to Columbus, Ohio and now, in December, I had completed the next year budget for Lee Middleton Original Dolls and the turnaround with revenue and profitability growth that would begin to appear in 2004. I had fulfilled my contract and put the company into a situation in which I could step back and spend my time with my own family in Madison.

I knew that Rob and Candy would move back to Tennessee after he completed his four year residency and I recognized that by my choosing to make a career change—one that would allow me the time and flexibility to be with loved ones—I would be taking advantage of a once-in-a-lifetime opportunity that wouldn't appear again. I didn't know what I would do professionally; that wasn't the issue at that time.

When January came around, I sat down to work out what I could do to satisfy my continuing need to be in the business world in a way that would not interfere with my free choice of time to be spent with my family. I began by writing a business plan to become a consultant. In doing internet research to develop my business plan, I came across *business coaching*. At the time, the term was relatively new. Not knowing what it meant, I dug deeper and discovered an organization called ActionCOACH Business Coaching; the company had, in the past couple of years, launched into the United States and it was an Australian company; that got my attention to a greater level! I dug more and learned that business coaching, and specifically, ActionCOACH, was a model that was aligned to my personal style of executive influence. As it was a franchise business, I could be my own business owner as a Franchisee; an owner for the first time since my years with SPASM!

I think many people believe that a business coach simply tells you what to do. This couldn't be further from the truth. A business coach asks the right questions in order to help a business owner, CEO or executive leader come to their best conclusions for themselves. This is what I came to understand during six weeks of diligence in research.

> **"***I think many people believe that a business coach simply tells you what to do. This couldn't be further from the truth.* **"**

The most powerful element of ActionCOACH that convinced me that it was the right franchise company for me was the vision of the founder, Bradley J. Sugars, "World Abundance Through Business Reeducation." These words summed up the connecting thought between ActionCOACH and my own approach to world betterment. I had a realization that this was a continuing path to legacy that began almost forty years earlier in the East-West Center and in the contrasting streets and palaces of India.

I joined ActionCOACH as a Franchisee in the state of Wisconsin on my sixty-fourth birthday in March of 2004.

After signing my papers, the next step I needed to complete was to attend a ten-day training session on how to be a coach (versus a consultant) that was held in Las Vegas (ActionCOACH Headquarters). As my plane landed in Las Vegas after my trip from Madison to begin the ten days of training, I checked my cell phone at the airport. There was a message from my son, Jeff, who at the time was in the U.S. Marine Corps. He'd just received his orders to go to Iraq to fight in the battle of Fallujah. I'd never had that feeling of loss of control before. My first reaction was to want to get back on the plane and go home. I decided to continue to the training as I realized that my not continuing with the business coaching in my life would in no way change Jeff's responsibility as a serviceman. Today, I couldn't be more grateful for that decision. The ActionCOACH training was powerful in its own right as it focused on challenging my purpose and the reason why I had decided to become a business coach. It also taught the technical aspects of how to be a coach, a new career for me.

In project-based consulting, success is dependent upon transferring and controlling technical and operational directives to the client. After that, the job is finished and the relationship, itself, is often no longer necessary or maintained. Business coaching involves asking a range of questions to influence the business owner/leader to actually come up with solutions themselves. Coaching continues in an experiential and relational manner while using business tools and systems to influence and inspire the business owner to make better decisions for business results, as well as for mindset growth at a personal level.

This style of business coaching, as opposed to consulting, took me all the way back to the principle of delegation on my great uncle's sheep farm. Later, in my extensive sporting activities, I was rarely the best, but I did have the ability to lead others to exemplify their gifts. This was also my style as a CEO executive in the many companies I had led. Delegation, influence, and inspiration are far more powerful in leading people than typical dictatorial ordering of their activities.

My ActionCOACH training and a number of lifelong friends have been with me ever since those first ten days in Las Vegas. Coaching continues to influence my own personal growth while I strive to be an influencer for others. When I was getting into leadership and business coaching, I realized that ActionCOACH was about the activity and process of coaching, and not the teaching of technical content. I needed to be a listener who worked with business leaders on how to get them to use their own acquired technical knowledge and information. However, I did find I could be most effective when I selectively helped them with experiences from my own background.

> *"I needed to be a listener who worked with business leaders."*

When my son and his family left for Tennessee after four years in Madison (they had added another son during that time), I decided to be more aggressive in looking for new, larger clients. To do this, I needed to provide documented credibility of my experiences and successes as a business leader and coach to let them know why I was the coach to help them grow.

'How __did__ I operate when I was leading and growing businesses myself as a CEO/owner?'

I realized that I had a process I'd always used even though I had never written it down.

- o Upfront – Vision and strategy
- o Next – Operations to achieve the strategy
- o Measure – Consistently and routinely measure financial results in business
- o Influence and inspiration – Develop staff to drive success

Because of what I'd learned from coaching experiences (which made me more conscious of developing people as a critical element to growth), I had to *write down* the plan/process that I'd been living since my first foray into the workforce with Heinz in 1965.

I had always worked to build positive employees and leaders who wanted to come to work, to have fun, to feel productive and to be able to express themselves personally. This was *culture*. Every company has culture. I decided that there had to be a recognition for organizational culture that related to each specific organization.

The next piece from coaching that I developed was to create *executive coaching* for Leadership Development as an extension of business coaching. Business coaching, in my mind, is important for the operations of the company; executive coaching is important for the development of the people and the leaders running the company.

Business is process; process is managed through people.

All business starts with WHY and ends with LEGACY. [Simon Sinek has written a great book titled, "START with WHY" – it is well worth reading.] When I finished writing down what I'd been living in my professional (and, honestly, personal) life for the decades before ActionCOACH, I realized I already had my coaching model. All of these pieces together—Purpose/WHY, process (strategic and operational planning toward desired financial results), culture and people development (at the team and leadership level), and ultimately, legacy—are what made up my map for success. I called this my <u>I</u>ntegrated <u>B</u>usiness <u>G</u>rowth <u>P</u>rocess, or **IBGP**.

IBGP is an annual cycle driven by the fact that it is required (by the Government – taxes!) to report annual financials. Operationally, these measurements relate to measuring effective financial results for each business.

> "*It is critical to know how to pull all of the operational information together as an annualized disciplined process.*"

How does IBGP work? That is the critical issue. There will always be some luck in every success. However, no one can depend on luck; it is important . . . nay . . . it is critical to know how to pull all of the operational information together as an annualized disciplined process.

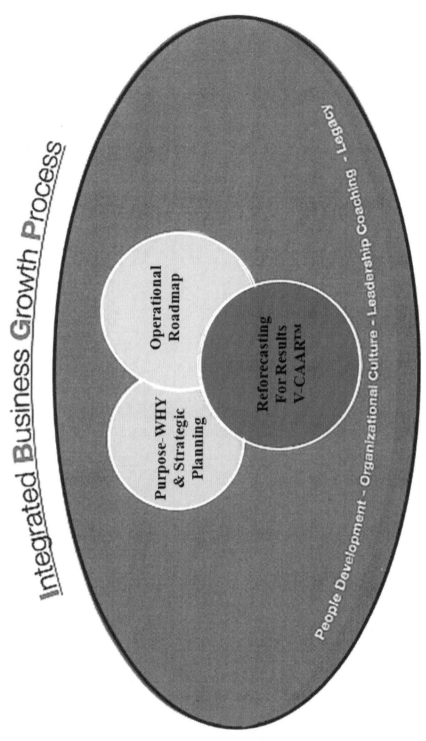

Legacy

Legacy can be something we purposefully drive toward or it can happen by accident; make no mistake, it will exist whether it is controlled or whether it is random.

When I moved to the U.S. permanently from Australia in January 1978 with the advertising agency Doyle Dane Bernbach (DDB) in New York City to head up Polaroid International advertising, Polaroid was the market innovator and leader without competition for instant photography. About this time, Kodak entered the instant photography market. Polaroid appropriately increased advertising and the availability of new products in instant photography. Their focus was to make it as difficult as possible for Kodak's entry into their marketplace. (Polaroid also filed legal action against Kodak for patent violation – however, this was really a side note to the marketplace operations).

At DDB, we submitted a strategic opportunity to leverage Polaroid technologies in order to diversify the company's product base. For example, the SX-70 auto focus camera, launched in the latter 1970s, had breakthrough technology in the automatic focusing of the lens. It used the time of a sound wave to the subject and bounce back to the camera in order to determine the focus; the time it took controlled the drive mechanism in the camera to set the focal length.

We formally recommended additional uses for the technology for product consideration:

- o Rear bumpers for cars in the auto-industry to determine distance while backing up o Create a device to help blind people determine distances to objects

We were told by Dr. Edwin Land, the Founder, that Polaroid was *"an instant photography, instant photography, instant photography company!"*

Dr. Land had always surrounded himself with the brightest minds of new graduates from top U.S. women's colleges across the nation to support him in his research projects; like so many inventors and geniuses, he often worked around the clock; he needed a large team to keep up with him. This team selected for their own intellectual capacities had to sign on to be available twenty-four/seven to visualize, research, create and implement Land's ideas. He was the leading inventor (and, quite frankly, a genius) at this time in the U.S. Land had more than five-hundred patents to his name. In our strategic product recommendations we had hoped to leverage his genius to diversify the company past photography. Beyond the auto-focus technology, he had a number of other valuable inventions that were in play as part of the instant photography product line:

  o He created the chemistry to allow for the process of in-camera film development.
  o He invented the flat battery to go into every film pack to drive power to the camera.
  o He had even invented instant home movie film capabilities (Polarvision).

It was disappointing, from both a commercial and a creative standpoint, that there wasn't an open mind to develop Land's brilliant discoveries for impacts beyond instant photography. At the time, and still today, I also respected Dr. Land for his innovative technical genius. I also respected him for his philosophical mind, much like so many of the world's greatest inventors and geniuses. His unwillingness to have an open mind to others ideas was surprising in this light.

The end result of Polaroid's stagnation was their lack of realization of the potential market impact of the introduction of digital photography and digital video . . . leaving Polaroid out of this new market opportunity. Polaroid never reacted because of the vision of being *"an instant photography, instant photography, instant photography company!"* (Incidentally, not learning from the lessons of Polaroid, Kodak also didn't adapt when the world moved to a digital transformation. Canon and Nikon took over.)

While the legacy of Land (and Polaroid) began as one of innovation, it ended with a company that essentially died with an era.

In the early 1980s, Dr. Land was removed from the Polaroid Board of Directors. As compensation the Company provided him with a research lab and staff in which he could research and create whatever he desired with any patents to be in Polaroid's name. The narrow focus of a genius mind allowed a breakthrough in the marketplace; the narrow focus on a rival and the lack of strategic market vision resulted in ultimate commercial losses.

Polaroid stands out as a primary example of a company with a default legacy . . . and Kodak, similarly.

Putting together a *purposeful* plan that captures the vision, the operations and the measurement of results with respect to the process and the people (as well as the culture in which they operate), is the IBGP.

The IBGP is an annual cycle working toward an overall legacy. The measurements relate to the requirements of business. Understanding how each of the individual elements of the IBGP work as activities as well as an integrated process is vital to its successful implementation.

ooooooooo

Purpose

The first step I take with the owner/leadership team is to identify Purpose. Every year, when looking forward (PRESENT-FUTURE Mindset, of course), we ask the question in the context of the long-term vision: *"do we need to streamline our **strategy** to stay successful over the next couple of years?"* It is a comfortable time period that is not threatening for forward, strategic thinking for the small to mid-sized companies I typically work with.

At the beginning of the second quarter, we spend two days OFF-SITE (so that the Team can get OUT OF the business) with key ownership and then with their executive team to go through this two year strategic thinking process.

However, before developing strategic plans, it is important to step back to look forward. Some call it vision; I prefer to ask, "What is the purpose of your business and why?" The reason I do this exercise with my clients is because the (concept of) VISION is used in such different and broad ways in cultural communications. I want business leaders to focus on *building their business through people*: are they aligned with the owner's/leadership purpose and why? This is a reflection that needs to be considered once a year.

Why do you own or run a business?

What are you trying to achieve?

What are your expectations for results?

Everyone is totally different and that's the fun part of it. We step back and jointly reflect. We say, "This is where we're at. Are we still consistent with our purpose?"

> **"***Everyone is totally different and that's the fun part of it. We step back and jointly reflect.* **"**

Hopefully, a *purpose* doesn't change very often. It's in you. Something may CAUSE change, such as my Asia and India trip that led me from wanting to only donate and philosophize versus desiring active change through economic resources. We need to understand changes, yet—while approaches evolve—the heart of our purposes should remain the same. Purpose is an internal drive. Depending on the person and the business, these considerations may be three-year to five-year goals considering the rapid rate of change pervading the world today. It may even be longer depending on the industry the business is in e.g. long term development and capital intensive versus shorter term retail.

Once the forward looking purpose of a company is reconfirmed as an annual process, the next step in the process is to start asking strategically about the following year. The reason this occurs in the second quarter of the current year is because I want the owner and key executives to feel their flow for the current year after three months of activities and of their operations before thinking in detail into the next year.

Typical strategic questions need to be asked:

"Where do you want the business to be at the end of next year?"

For example:

o *Will the company be in the same markets?*
o *Are there any new market opportunities?*
o *Will the products be the same?*
o *Is there a need for innovation or researched and developed (R&D) products?*
o *What are the results of analyses and industry financial forecasts?*
o *How do futures look for local, regional, and national economies?*

o *What external (and internal) contexts could impact the business?*

Given where you are forecasting financially to be at the end of this current year, where do you want to be at the end of the next year. For example, what is required regarding:

o *Rate of growth?*
o *Staffing/Organizational structure?*
o *Market penetration?*
o *Profitability?*
o *Cash flow?*

With a first quarter of operations behind the business, the Management team is now operating in a sense of knowing how they're tracking towards this year's planned results.

Developing strategic goals is the relatively fun part of the IBGP. However, implementing these goals requires a detailed and budgeted Operational Roadmap. This roadmap is created at approximately mid-third quarter to the early fourth quarter and will end up with next year's approved budget by the end of November (or the appropriate date dictated by the nature of each business). With more data available by the time of this Operational Roadmapping exercise, leaders can be more specific for developing next year's budget. Once again, I usually encourage my clients to spend two days offsite for this critical annual step to be able to see the picture away from day-to-day disruptions.

oooooooo

Strategic plan plots course to firm's goal

By Iain Macfarlane in the Capital Region Business Journal, Madison, Wisconsin

Strategic planning is the most important function of a CEO or Business Owner. It identifies where a company wants to be at a defined point of time in the future and what actions it is going to take to get there. Strategic Planning is critical to the growth and success of every company. And if the company has a Board of Directors, a formal strategic planning process enables the Board to have a significant impact on the company's overall direction and on-going performance. For a company of any size, strategic planning is the "roadmap" to future success.

The strategic aspect of the planning process is to understand the current operating and performance situation of the company and the relationship to the outside business environment, the vision and mission of the company as identified by the executive management of the company, the resources and structure to achieve the roadmap goals, and the summary of how the outcome strategic plan will impact the future of the company. The structure of the strategic plan is designed to carry out strategic thinking, direction, and action that lead to the achievement of consistent and planned results.

Consequently, having skills to execute the planning process for any company is critical to the long term viability and success of the company. The process of planning includes the selection of the planning team, clarification of team member roles, careful structuring of the planning meetings, and the guiding of the team through the process itself.

In embracing the importance of strategic planning to achieve both short term (one to three years) and longer term (three to five years) results, there are four key issues to recognize:

1. It is essential that the process be led by the owner or CEO and that the executives and managers in the company understand and use the planning process.
2. There must be an organizational commitment to both the planning process and the implementation of the plan; all of the participants in the process must see the benefits to themselves personally as well as to the company as a whole.

3. The planning process is as important, if not more important, than the content of the plan itself.

4. The planning process is never done. It is part of the overall process of managing the company and the planning process is an ongoing process rather than an annual event.

The strategic plan focuses on the basic nature (Purpose/Why) and direction (strategy) of the organization. The operational plan concentrates on how to implement the strategic plan and produce short-term results. The performance management aspect of the process is concerned with comparing performance with plan (both strategic and financial) and ensuring the achievement of forecasted results. Even though each component serves a different purpose, each of the components is fully integrated with the other.

The strategic plan must be seen as a living document clearly communicated throughout the company and should not be a "fluffy" document that ends up collecting dust on a shelf and wasted time and energy in its development. The purpose of planning is not to produce plans, it is to produce results. A strategic plan needs to be the result of a productive process of committed executives led by the business owner or CEO of any sized business to provide the thinking and planning for the future success of the company, that allows for the detailed operational planning to achieve short term outcome results, and defines measurement performance criteria representing the long term success goals for the company.

No company has the option to simply hope that it will be successful; every company must have *a management committed and disciplined process* of strategic planning to create a roadmap to both short term and long term business and financial success.

ooooooo

"No company has the option to simply hope that it will be successful."

The Operational Roadmap developed around the end of the Third Quarter is based on the strategy previously developed for the next financial year and is reconfirmed prior to beginning the Operational Roadmap planning If that's where we want to be, what **assumptions** do we need to make operationally regarding profitability, revenues, margins, marketing, administrative expenses, capital needs, etc.; what are the planned key performance indicators such as leads, conversion rates, average transactions, number of transactions per client, and all other related numbers. Assumptions for next year are based on internal and external factors that have occurred in the first eight to nine months of the current year (Past-Present analysis). There now must be detailed assumptions about what needs to be done to take the business forward successfully. We may know where the current revenue is tracking, but how does the leadership plan for growth? What changes have to be made to the Operational plan (roadmap)? This will be a PRESENT-FUTURE Mindset.

Each assumption should have a related action plan.

How do you improve the gross margin?

What needs to be done to improve marketing effectiveness?

What are the appropriate expense levels: go through every expense line item to determine what is fixed, what is variable, and how both areas can be worked with.

The two most common key areas of forward-looking expenses with variation are:

1. People (staffing / skills / organizational structure)
2. Marketing

These two areas will be critical to the rate of growth planned for the business over the next one to two years.

oooooooo

People

With a forecast for revenue growth, you need to decide what is required for new people skills to facilitate the planned rate of growth. When we're growing, we will almost certainly need to make people adjustments.

Leaders should ask:

Do we currently have the right people with the right skills?

Do we have any gaps in the current staffing related to functional needs for business growth?

Do we have any redundancies?

What technical and people development training will be needed to "grow the business through people"?

The best way to analyze whether there are gaps (or, conversely, redundancy) in people is to create a Functional Chart which feeds INTO formalizing the organizational chart.

Beyond day-to-day production and functionality requirements to grow a company there will always be more longer term requirements that will need to be assessed at least annually. Start with the following examples of Functions as categories (the functions will vary by company related to the type and size of the company's business):

- o Human Resources
- o Legal
- o Sales
- o Marketing (Yes – Sales and Marketing are DIFFERENT!)
- o Production
- o Distribution and Delivery
- o Facilities Maintenance
- o Administration

Next, identify each and every operations activity under each Function category previously identified for the specific company.

The executive team assigns employee names (initials) to each operational activity identified. Then it can be determined in any growth business where staffing gaps exist related to identified operational needs. Additionally, there may be multiple sets of initials for specific activities where a single employee could be assigned to the activity. And in many cases, some employees initials appear everywhere indicating they may be spread too thin to be fully effective in areas that they have been employed to fulfill.

This analysis helps to confirm the staffing needed to execute the operating assumptions for the next year through people. Leaders also identify and learn, through exercises like this one, that there may be training needs. How much more should be budgeted for training? The assumptions come back to impacting the financials and we ultimately ask again: "what is the financial impact to the business?"

In effect, seeing people through the lens of functions and organization structure sets the vision for a business's people needs and the ramifications on its ability to operate effectively and to maximize financial performance.

The value and quality of the budget isn't the numbers; the effectiveness of the budget as a tool is based on the thinking you put into the **assumptions** that allow you to create the numbers in the budget. The budget is merely the output of the assumptions. Accountants frequently struggle with that concept.

> "*The value of the budget isn't in the numbers, but on the thinking you put into the assumptions that allow you to create the budget.*"

It's not numbers; it's the **thinking** that creates the numbers with a PRESENT-FUTURE Mindset!

oooooooo

Marketing

In reality, marketing can be defined as "*communications effectiveness*". It's how a company relays its vision or message to other businesses (B2B), to end user customers (B2C), and internally (TEAM). Marketing needs to be specifically designed to positively impact each individual target audience identified; it is the tangible reflection of purpose.

The question to be answered for marketing is, "how can we IMPACT people (target audience) to generate positive measureable results?"

Some companies have traditional advertising media including some elements of digital advertising but don't understand the differences between advertising and effective marketing. When thinking into the next year, the question to ask is: "what is a better way next year to communicate our market position to our target audiences with more effective *impact* than we did this past year?" If we want to grow, our marketing will probably need to increase as it will be a driver of our top line growth.

When I worked with the innovative and breakthrough marketing communication company in 1987-1988 based in Knoxville, Tennessee, Whittle Communications, I was responsible for handling Procter & Gamble (P&G) custom communications that included our first assignment, Crest Toothpaste. Our proposal to P&G top management (we went in at a level above Marketing and Advertising) was we could design a new marketing approach (results to be measured by Nielsen Market Share) that would increase their sales volume for the same cost as the last five million dollars of their traditional advertising budget ($125 million at that time) and knowing they had no way to know what the measurable impact was from the last five million dollars of their $125 million traditional TV advertising.

We had developed an innovative idea internally and did market research to provide sufficient validation for P&G to agree to our proposal that included a three year contract. The key question we asked ourselves was to identify the most important target audience for Crest Toothpaste and where would be the best place to find them and to influence them.

The answer was above average income customers and with a strong interest in dental care. Where could we find them on a targeted basis? Answer: dental office waiting rooms where the customer could afford the dentist cost and they obviously had an interest in dental care. The average waiting time was more than twenty minutes.

We created and designed a colorful large wall poster in a frame that got attention by having a featured public personality with some of their quotes about dental care and other fun facts about dentistry e.g. *"where and when was dentistry first practiced?"* (In Egypt, by the way, in approximately 2900 BC!) On the side of the poster we had ten small brochure pockets, each with interesting and informative information on ten aspects of dental care. We consumer tested these materials in focus groups (took me back to 1967 at Heinz in Australia where I first used this technique for measuring effectiveness of consumer communications) to maximize the effectiveness of the consumer communications.

Our biggest issue: How could we convince dentists to allow us to put these materials on the walls of their dental offices? (At this time there were 32,000 dental offices nationally.)

Solution: We built a fee into our business model to pay dentists for the space we would use that included replacing the primary poster with a new personality once per Quarter.

Outcome: To our surprise our sales presentation to the test dentist offices we used was so appealing to the dentists as a form of both informing an entertaining their patients with the fun wall posters, they took the promotion without requiring any space fees! (Higher profit margin for us than we had anticipated.) Over the next couple of years Crest gained an increased market share of over two percent and this was a significant direct measureable payback and **R**.eturn **O**.n I.nvestment (ROI) for the annual five million dollar cost.

In the "Purpose – WHY and Strategic Streamlining" planning of the IBGP, companies should challenge themselves in their forward thinking, their PRESENT-FUTURE Mindset; COULD their planning identify better opportunities for growth? How could their current strategic approach be modified?

At the heart of the Integrated Business Growth Process is a leader who can guide the purpose, communicate the operational roadmap, maintain his own executive level of coaching in order to develop people and reflect organizational culture, and strive toward legacy.

To recap the Purpose/WHY and strategic streamlining overview of the IBGP:

- o Identify a **LEGACY** in order to prevent a default legacy
- o Leaders identify the **PURPOSE** (WHY) and tie it to a strategic, streamlined process that focuses on the areas of:
  - o People
  - o Marketing/Sales
  - o Financial performance metrics

- o Market innovation
- o Leaders should receive **EXECUTIVE COACHING** in order to be purposeful about:
  - O PEOPLE DEVELOPMENT
  - O ORGANIZATIONAL CULTURE
- o The overall process should be done according to a repeatable annual cycle

The remaining two core elements of the Integrated Business Growth Process include an *OPERATIONAL ROADMAP* in which the next year's annual plans laid out are converted to numbers; and the monthly *V-CAAR*™ which continuously measures and reforecasts results to create accountability to purpose and track toward the legacy. We'll look at each of these areas in more detail in the next two Chapters. Before those breakdowns, you may wish to read more about IBGP elements and the role of the leader within them.

For more on the *leadership*, the center of the IBGP, check out these Capital Region Business Journal articles: *"It Can be Lonely at the Top"*(from March 2008), *"To Motivate Others, First Look in the Mirror"* (from September 2006), *"Easy Ways to Become a Better Leader"* (from January 2006), and *"Don't Confuse Ownership and Leadership"* (from May 2005).

To dig deeper in the area of *people development*, my Capital Region Business Journal articles, *"Hiring a Staff vs. Building a Team"* (from December 2007) and *"Six Rules to Maximize Your Team"* (from March 2006), are also quality resources. Please note the websites for these articles on the next page, or simply scan the QR codes for the different articles.

"It Can be Lonely at the Top"

https://goo.gl/xcYF2A

"Don't Confuse Ownership and Leadership"

https://goo.gl/VpF1tS

"To Motivate Others, First Look in the Mirror"

https://goo.gl/l8vFHe

"Hiring a Staff vs. Building a Team"

https://goo.gl/Oko6m8

"Easy Ways to Become a Better Leader"

https://goo.gl/0UVs58

"Six Rules to Maximize Your Team"

https://goo.gl/P2GFcI

So You Can Work Toward Your Purpose, Consider These Questions:

1. What is your purpose as the Owner and/or Leader for building the business?

2. What is it your personal WHY for owning/leading/ being in this business? WHY did you start/get into the business?

3. What bigger community impact are you trying to achieve through the business purpose?

*"How can we impact **people**

to generate positive,

measurable results?"*

~I.M.

The Power of an Operational Roadmap

. . . So You Can Work with Process

"The reason why most people face the future with apprehension instead of anticipation is because they don't have it well designed."

~Jim Rohn, Entrepreneur, Author and
Motivational Speaker

*T*he Operational Roadmap is a conversion of the operating assumptions into actual **Action Planning** for the next year; this is the basis for putting financial numbers into the proposed budget.

If leaders start work in September, and work with an executive team on an iterative basis, they may rethink assumptions if the actions and the financial numbers are not aligning with one another; if next year's draft budget is not meeting acceptable expectations. The exchange goes back and forth until the beginning of December when final decisions and commitments are made to the next annual budget. Activities and Action Plans are needed to achieve the strategic exercise developed earlier in the year . . . following this process will give you a "Straight-A Budget"!

The Power of the Budget is the disciplined development of the operating assumptions and related Action Plans; the financial numbers are only an output, the conversion to dollars and cents, of the assumptions.

ooooooo

Avoid the "better mousetrap" syndrome when starting a business

By Iain Macfarlane in the Capital Region Business Journal, Madison, Wisconsin

As highly successful college football coach Lou Holtz said, "Most people fail because they fail to understand what they are trying to do."

When entrepreneurs start a business, their personal desire may be clear, but the clarity of their business vision is usually clouded by their passion, their energy, their willingness to be a risk-taker and their sincere belief that they can do it better than anyone else. The hard reality of statistics as reported by the Small Business Administration is that:

- o Sixty-six percent of new employer businesses survive at least two years
- o Forty-four percent survive at least four years, and
- o Twenty percent will survive five years
- o Of the twenty percent that survive the first five years, only twenty percent will survive the second five years

In other words, only four percent of businesses survive the first ten years of operation. The fundamental first step to being successful is to understand the reason or reasons you are starting the business. Such understanding requires knowing the difference between building a business and just creating a job.

Too often, businesses fail because the owner, with his or her entrepreneurial excitement, feels that their own passion is shared by others. **To start a successful business, the market must be large enough to build a profitable business.**

Another start-up consideration is to make sure business goals are aligned to the owner's personal goals. Too often, the business owner gets so caught up in day-to- day operations, they lose contact with the reasons that led them to starting the business in the first place. If the business does not let you achieve personal goals, why would you go into business?

Create a business plan

The solution is a well thought-out and realistic business plan, a roadmap to building the business. The business plan helps to focus on goals, identify action plans and achieve planned results. It provides a tool to measure the level of success in building the business, and it helps identify the need to make changes based on actual market performance.

For start-up or early stage companies in Madison where I live, there are a number of electronic business plan templates that can be purchased at bookstores or online. The UW Business School in Madison and the Southwest Wisconsin Small Business Development Center offer a number of excellent short-term programs for entrepreneurs to prepare them at this early decision-making process of starting a new business.

Reasons for failure

The main reasons for small business failures, according to several studies, are:

o Poor management
o Lack of business experience
o Ineffective leadership

New business owners frequently lack relevant business, management and leadership experience in areas such as finance, cash flow budgeting and forecasting, purchasing, production, marketing, selling, advertising, public relations, customer service, hiring and managing employees, market research and analysis, or some combination of these vital areas.

Unless the owner recognizes what they don't do well, and therefore invests in seeking appropriate help, they will face business problems quickly. Even as success occurs, it will always be important to continually measure against the goals of the business. Planning and execution are critical to success.

Unfortunately, the passion, the energy, the enthusiasm, the willingness to be a risk-taker, and the belief in oneself as an entrepreneur can override the need for financial knowledge, planning and execution skills that are critical to the success of every business.

Hope and passion can inspire people to be a part of a business, but they do not pay the bills of the business.

The hope that the better mousetrap will automatically build a business is too prevalent among entrepreneurs. This frequently leads to poor record keeping, a lack of financial controls, little to no accountability to financial requirements, and missed regulatory compliances and other business filings. With poor financial management, there is the common and frequently fatal mistake of having insufficient operating funds and working capital.

Business owners consistently underestimate how much money is needed to cover their planned operations and the unknown changes that will occur as they get into the marketplace. It is not just the cost of starting the business; it is the cost of continuing the business. A leading cause of failure is over-expansion, which can happen when business owners confuse success with how fast they can expand their business.

A rule of thumb is that the entrepreneur should be able to live for the first two years without any income from the business.

Outside advice is often needed for developing and challenging the detailed financial assumptions of the business covering operations for the first three years of the business.

Get outside advice

The financial assumptions, in particular, need to be challenged by outsiders who have operations and industry experience that relate to the entrepreneur's proposed business. This financial data will be integrated with the business plan that must be developed for any new or ongoing business.

Reinforcing the principle that start-up business plan finances will initially tend to be over-optimistic is reflected in the way venture capitalists tend to evaluate new business plan finances presented to them for potential funding:

FIRST – They cut the revenue in half.

SECOND – They double the time to success proposed by the entrepreneur.

THIRD – They examine the viability of the business plan.

FOURTH – They assess the skills of the entrepreneur.

Entrepreneurs made the United States (and, I might add, Australia) great countries. New entrepreneurs can achieve success by:

- Being aware of obvious business and personal mistakes to avoid
- Planning a business model that is financially realistic on a twelve-month forecast consistent with a three-year business vision
- Breaking operating tactics into ninety-day segments
- Not trying to go it alone

If these guidelines are followed, it should not be difficult to dramatically improve the current new business success rates of only four percent survival rate past the first ten years from launch.

An Operational Roadmap has its value in the numbers; however, it is more likely to prove successful when a strategic thought process is applied to the operational process. In 1997, after being recruited to execute a turnaround for book publishing company Cowles Creative Publishing in Minneapolis—moving it from a direct mail marketing approach to include traditional book retailers—I initially began by moving the company from its niche direct mail influence to a general book distribution retail market with an international market potential.

I changed the company name to **Creative Publishing International**. The name change was very strategic, as was one of our project successes, *"Chased by the Light"*, authored by already established preeminent international photographer, Jim Brandenburg.

Brandenburg already had prestigious awards and accolades to his name. He was world-renowned for his photography of wolves, was routinely contracted by National Geographic as one of their top photographers, had been featured internationally in magazines, books, documentaries, and other media, and was already a repeat bestseller on numerous noteworthy lists. Nonetheless, he said he felt empty after his self-imposed retirement from National Geographic in the mid 1990s.

"I don't think that I was paying homage to the thing I started: a very quiet, contemplative, personal relationship with nature."

To reawaken his personal passion for his art, he sought a ninety-day journey, from fall to winter, in which—each day—he would take only one single picture . . . only one click of the button per day . . . one capture of the moment per day. He took his self-assigned task seriously. This was Brandenburg's chance to prove **to himself** that he could do a "live performance." Typically, in his National Geographic photographer's role, he had been accustomed to taking from hundreds to thousands of pictures a day while selecting just a small percentage for print production. That's not what this challenge was going to be about.

Brandenburg owned 1,500 acres on the pristine and protected Boundary Waters between north-east Minnesota and Canada where he was going to build his dream home. Of Norwegian heritage, it was important for him to be by northern waters. Two years after his retirement, National Geographic reached out to him to see what he'd been doing.

He hadn't done much photography outside of the ninety-day personal challenge he'd given himself; he had been concentrating on building his dream home. They looked at the photos and said, "Jim! This is spectacular!" They wanted to run it in National Geographic; he was given the cover and, uniquely for National Geographic, they allowed him to write his own editorial for that issue and it was one of the top-selling National Geographic magazines. Realizing the well-received nature of the project he decided to put it into a book although this had never been his intention when started his ninety-day personal challenge.

As far as traditional photographic books go, after I started publishing discussions with Jim, I realized this was so much bigger than the quality of the pictures; it was the uniqueness of the challenge that had never been done before by any of the world's great photographers. *It was the discipline of only taking one picture per day in real life outdoor situations including moving animals and birds and in different light conditions **and** not seeing the result until the whole ninety-day project was finished.*

When I explained to Brandenburg that this was really a book about a personal challenge rather than the quality of the technical photographic work (which was of the sort of inspirational awe one would expect from a world-renowned National Geographic photographer), he understood the strategic approach very quickly for publishing this book.

We launched the book around Jim Brandenburg the person and the unique personal challenge within the book.

Brandenburg admits that the initial project was just "for him" and, once developed, the ninety-day work sat in a drawer for two years. However, after the public recognition in the National Geographic issue convinced him to turn it into a book, *"Chased by the Light"*, a coffee table book priced at $35.00, it sold over 200,000 copies and became Brandenburg's bestselling 'photography' book ever. (A coffee table photographic book from a leading photographer would normally sell less than 10,000 copies at best.)

Jim Brandenburg was able

Jim Brandenburg at home on the Boundary Waters.

to impact the environmental causes that mattered most to him with the financial results of this book and, importantly, reignite his passion for photography.

"Chased by the Light" applied a strategic thought process to what had started out as an operational process. It is the marrying of strategic thought, operational planning and planned financial results that together create the Operational Roadmap piece of the IBGP.

Iain's copy is inscribed:

> *"For Iain, I cannot thank you enough for your vision and support, but most importantly, your friendship. I hope you are as proud as I am of this story - you were a crucial part of its publication! With deepest respect,*
>
> *Jim Brandenburg, Ely"*

The lesson of Brandenburg's book is to never accept the normal. Challenge the normal because maybe there's a better approach . . . a better roadmap toward success and the resulting numbers. Look at projects to find exceptional ways of doing them and be willing to be vulnerable and take risks.

ooooooo

With the purposeful strategy of developing opportunities for international publishing at Creative Publishing International, I took on a unique and potentially controversial international publishing project in 1998 – to publish a photo biography of the Shah of Iran in the Farsi language. This project was on behalf of relatives and friends of the Shah. As the content of the book was to be based on already publicly published photos and related editorial content, I felt comfortable in my taking on this project as a personal 'out of my comfort zone' challenge.

A number of Iranian academics and political exiles lived in Paris. Through Iranian contacts in the U.S., I was able to make contact with some of these Iranian expatriates in Paris, including Queen Farah who was the wife of the Shah and who was living under the protection of the French Government (the Shah had died in 1980). I also had international publisher contacts including one in France who had the experience of publishing photo biographies.

With interested contacts lined up I made a trip to Paris. Before leaving on this trip I met with the Shah's son and heir who endorsed this project. My first meeting in Paris was with the French publisher who had previously worked with a number of Iranians in publishing books in Farsi. We laid out a specific publishing plan and he introduced me to contacts who could do the research of photographs and compile the photos into an historical journal. We also met with academics willing to research the background of each photo and describing the context of each photo.

During my week in Paris, the most critical meeting was a day with Queen Farah in her highly secured apartment reviewing the final plan and details of the publication. At the end of the day we went to dinner at her favorite (highly guarded) restaurant with six other exiled Iranians who had escaped Iran in the 1979 revolution and some had served in Cabinet positions of the Shah's government. At one point during the dinner when the Iranians were conversing in Farsi, Queen Farah turned to me and apologized for this situation and said, "You wouldn't want to know what we are talking about!"

As someone unfamiliar with Iran except for a trip to Tehran prior to the Shah's overthrow, I was surprised at the progressive approach the Shah had taken during his reign. Iran had been under continuous monarchy for 2,500 years since the founding of the Persian Empire. Shah Reza Pahlavi came to power in Iran after the abdication of his father in 1941. He introduced the "White Revolution" which was a series of economic, social and political reforms with the intention of transforming Iran into a global power with modernization.

The Shah was a secular Muslim who gradually lost support from the Shi'a clergy due to his strong policy of modernization, secularization and relations with Israel. However, he also had corruption issues surrounding himself, his family and the ruling elite. Other factors leading to his eventual overthrow in 1979 were clashes with traditional Islamists, the support for his regime from the U.S. and UK, his banning of the Communist Party and political dissent from his Intelligence Agency. In the 1970s, his clashes with Islamists and communists led to massive arrests of political prisoners and this led to his final overthrow from internal revolt.

As a parting gift for my leadership in this publishing project Queen Farah gave me a Dupont pen engraved with the Shah's Crown of Persia. The printing and distribution of the book was based in Paris with most of the book sales occurring in France, UK and U.S.

My lesson from this project was the reinforcement of doing operational road mapping with people who had the knowledge and technical skills to make my 'out of comfort zone' project happen successfully.

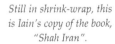

Still in shrink-wrap, this is Iain's copy of the book, "Shah Iran".

Operational planning can help your company achieve its goals

By Iain Macfarlane in the Capital Region Business Journal, Madison, Wisconsin

Developing an operational plan, including a budget for the upcoming year, tends to be a daunting task for most companies.

During the Fourth Quarter when next year's operational plan needs to be finalized, this process occurs at the same time that management is focusing on the maximizing of the business performance in the current year.

So, which is more important? In fact, they are equally important for the ongoing success of any business. Every business has some form of operational planning that is being executed currently, even if it is only in the minds of the business owner, CEO or one or more key managers.

However, effective operational planning requires formal acknowledgement of the need for a planning process. This process, involving key corporate and unit managers, requires:

o   Analysis of historical and current performance of the business.

o   Developing specific assumptions out of the analysis to be the basis for the next year's business objectives and goals.

o   Developing a financial budget that represents these assumptions and objectives.

o   Identifying what the Key Performance Indicators will be and how results will be measured.

Four key questions that need to be asked are:

1.   Is the current planning and budgeting process clearly identifying what needs to be accomplished for the business to be successful, operationally and financially?

2.   Does the plan lead to the implementation effort needed from all staff to produce the identified objectives and results?

3.   Does the plan development include all managers and key employees integrated both horizontally and vertically to increase staff motivation and the desire to meet targeted operating goals?

4.   Whatever planning process is currently being used, how can it be strengthened to achieve greater consistency in achieving targeted goals, to improve decision making, and to identify problems before they occur?

The Strategic Plan developed early in the Second Quarter of the current year identifies a roadmap for where a company wants to be at a defined point of time, usually *two to three years* out.

The Operational Roadmap developed by the end of the Third Quarter clearly documents what the company intends to accomplish in the *next year*, how and what Actions Plans will executed, who in the company will be accountable for these actions, and what the targeted results will be.

Most business owners and CEO's tend to have some idea of what financial results they are looking for in the upcoming year, and some will have put together a financial budget *by month*. However, these budgets will usually be made up of the current year's monthly historical performance with some sort of modification for the same month in the upcoming year's monthly budget. (This is a common accountant's approach to budgeting as they are, by nature, cautious, and prefer to use the certainty of historical results.)

Unfortunately, very few business owners and CEO's execute a *formalized and documented operational road mapping process* taking into account a specific exercise of detailed forward thinking strategic considerations. The typical approach is a process to provide the necessary information with year-to-year consistency and reliability to culminate in a budget for an *upcoming year*.

A budget developed on its own without considerations beyond working capital will rarely provide the basis to maximize financial performance over an upcoming year of operations. Some important benefits of implementing a strategic-based, forward-looking operational road mapping process include:

- o It provides a standardized management planning tool from year-to-year that can be used for both the total organization and for individual operating units

o It provides for the relationship of a broader longer term strategic 'roadmap' translated into achievable annual actions and identified business and financial measurable results

o It provides clear direction to managers and employees on both a horizontal and on a vertical basis to understand goals for the company in total and for their own unit, and how all these entities will have an impact on the company's total business results

o It allows the budget to be a more reliable management tool by taking into account forward planned operational issues rather than just make a monthly adjustment based on the prior year's monthly financial performance

o It will support strengthened team building throughout the company as managers and key employees will have been involved horizontally and vertically in the analyzing, planning and commitment to specific objectives and actions. And importantly, how the results will be measured.

Strategic planning and operational road mapping should be an ongoing annualized process for every company of any size. Measuring results must be a continuous process, annual updating of the company's two to three year strategic plan should take place in the first half of each year, usually during the Second Quarter. And operational road mapping should begin in the latter part of the third quarter to culminate in the upcoming year's approved budget in December of each year.

ooooooo

For more on the combination of strategic thought and operational and financial planning, read *"The Doing is the Thing"* originally published in the Capital Region Business Journal in February, 2007 at *https://goo.gl/qJpUvC* or simply scan the code at the right.

Iain Macfarlane

The Power of the V-CAAR™

... So You Can Analyze Your Journey

"I have been struck again and again by how important measurement is to improving the human condition."

~Bill Gates, Entrepreneur and Philanthropist

*I*n my first position as a Product Manager for Soup with H.J. Heinz in Pittsburgh in January 1965, Paul Townsend was the newly appointed Vice President of Marketing. The company had recently changed from an old-school sales focus to the new consumer marketing world. Paul had been recruited from Procter & Gamble with nine other marketing people to totally change the expertise and culture at Heinz (I was one of four additional non-P&G people brought into the new Marketing Department).

We celebrated all of the Nielsen market share reports when they came out as our results began to quickly improve. This fitted into the celebratory athletic and international cultures I had already experienced; it was my first exposure in the business world and I thought that was normal! **We had long days and many nights and weekends to bring about aggressive change to Heinz. I always had had energy that was** consistent with this "revolution" now happening at Heinz. These experiences reminded me of a quote I had read by Napoleon Hill, an authority on business history in the U.S.: "Desire is the starting point of all achievement, not a hope, not a wish, but a keen pulsating desire which transcends everything."

In reflecting back, I'm able to recognize just how lucky I was to be working in such a positive professional environment in the mid-1960s.

I loved work.

I was passionate about the opportunity.

So began a marathon of now fifty years

of collecting professional experiences.

When I transferred from Heinz, Pittsburgh to Heinz Australia in Melbourne in January 1967, I became the General Manager of Marketing and Business Development. I also taught undergraduate and graduate-level marketing programs at Monash University in the Faculty of Economics and Politics in evenings after work. I still to this day love teaching the principles of business and of life, particularly when based on my practical experiences and applications, rather than theory.

Even though my personality wasn't aligned with the educational process of universities at that time, I still wanted to share my knowledge. At universities in Australia, as an example, we were supposed to only give one set of three-hour exams at the end of each year. I was raising kids, teaching, working and playing cricket, so I decided to do multiple choice exams for the students throughout the year and a shorter end of year written exam (my Under-graduate class was over 300 students!). For the written exam at the end of the year, I would re-read the top and the bottom scores and random papers of student results after my two Graduate Assistants had marked the exam papers; this was to review for consistency and to see if any results could be different.

I was raked across the coals by other "traditional" teaching staff for not evaluating exam results "properly", i.e., I was not doing the test evaluations the way they had always been done in the past. The next thing, after all final exams, names and scores of all of the students had been compiled, the full teaching staff met together. Anyone with scores of fifty and above passed. If a student was below fifty in ANY course, the student failed the full year and had to retake. Each student had a maximum of twelve years to finish the full degree. I had an older woman student that I'd scored a forty-eight, but in her twelfth year. After being asked to change her score, I conceded and we moved her to a fifty to allow her to graduate (I was not going to stop a person from finally getting her degree after such a consistent, hard working effort with a great attitude – I had met her a few times after classes).

I taught a second year at Monash and then decided that the rules and regulations were not for me. It wasn't the teaching, it was the bureaucratic process and the red tape!

At the same time, I had a once in a lifetime experience with one of my students I taught in the graduate program. In his second year he was required to write a thesis under my guidance. His proposal was to write a business plan to launch a new company based on a Patent he had been issued a couple of years earlier. I approved his subject.

His simple idea for his patent came from reading about wine storage in ancient times in 'air tight' collapsible animal skin containers that poured from the bottom so air could not get in the top. His patent was for a sealed plastic bag with a "faucet" at the bottom to release the wine. It was "wine in a box" patent!!! He had a well written and documented thesis. I gave him an "A".

After graduation he and I had a long discussion about the practicality of launching his own company to build a wine packaging and distribution business. Not to discourage him but to give him an attractive option to consider, I suggested he license the patent to a packaging company with international capabilities. He contracted with an Australian company for a lucrative and long term licensing agreement. And "wine in a box" is now available in many parts of the world.

I'd also taken on a consulting job referred to me by Monash University. I was introduced to Eddie Baitz; he had incredible taste buds and could back-engineer liqueurs and tell exactly what ingredients were in them. He used his skill set to launch knock-offs of the most famous liqueurs. He was one of only six Masters (the only one in Australia) in the world for liqueur development and he always considered the possibility of doing better, of improving what was already on the market under his own brand label.

My role was to help Eddie understand the opportunities of marketing to grow his business. I worked with him for over a year and we launched two new liqueurs. And I learnt a lot, and appreciation, of liqueurs! My favorite was Gold Wasser with gold flakes in the liqueur!

During my five years with Heinz in Australia, I realized I wanted to be an entrepreneur. Natural products ("hippie era") were coming in, particularly clothing, etc. I had some clothes and other natural products designed and wanted to launch them in the U.S. in department stores. I had a range of products and my wife made a trip back to Detroit where she grew up. She made a visit to Hudson's and they were interested in the line. I also visited, just to sound them out, a department store in NY. It was fact finding, not sales.

I made a decision that I thought it would work. I gave Heinz six months notice. I got a letter from Tony O'Reilly who at the time was a leading executive of Heinz. From our sporting backgrounds I had developed a strong relationship with him. He was a great Rugby player from the late 1950s, the Irish 100 yards champion, rated as the number one orator in the UK. He had originally been recruited by Heinz to run Heinz UK. He later became CEO of Heinz worldwide. His personal letter to me was very complimentary and he told me that there would always be a position for me at Heinz.

During my time at Heinz we had been using Grey Advertising agency, a subsidiary of a large U.S. ad agency, for all basic products. I also used a local boutique ad agency for new products; not just for advertising but I also used them for market research to identify and understand what types of new products could be created in the food business.

In that time period, we tested the concept of what is now called FOCUS GROUPS for research. It was originally invented by Dr. Peter Kenny at the University of Sydney (a Professor of

Philosophy and a proponent of the Free Love Society . . . let's call him an open-minded philosopher!). He had started working with the advertising agency Singleton, Palmer & Strauss McAllan (SPASM) – four young guys who wanted to make advertising breakthroughs. John Singleton, one of the Partners, was a friend of Dr. Peter Kenny. Working with them we came up with a methodology of using focus groups to test out specific concept food products, as well as with advertising communication concepts to describe these specific new food ideas.

We introduced this testing in product development while I was at Heinz and further developed the methodology a few years later when I left Heinz to become a Partner at SPASM in Sydney; this was the methodology we used to help us become successful with the Pizza Hut marketing in Australia when they became a new client of SPASM. It was this innovative way of matching product development with advertising communications that convinced the original founder of Pizza Hut on a trip to Australia, Frank Carney, to give us their account.

When I announced in 1971 with six months notice that I would be leaving Heinz to start my own natural products company, I was approached by John Singleton who told me that SPASM was going to be broken into two new companies splitting between Sydney and Melbourne. I basically said I'd consider it but I was going to take enough time to develop my distribution of my natural products in the U.S. After consideration and rather than wait to get my own company off the ground, I joined John Singleton and Duncan McAllan as a Partner in Sydney. I became the business side of the ad agency

SPASM (NSW) and Singleton and McAllan were the creative side.

I brought in a lot of new business with my Heinz packaged goods marketing experiences in both the U.S. and Australia; and we grew quickly. With this quick growth we needed a lot more space. Three to four blocks away, there was a beautiful convict-built stone building from the early 1800s. We knew a young developer and we approached him about developing the building with us as an anchor tenant. It was on Palmer Street . . . the red light district of Sydney. We named the building "Squizzy Taylor Square." Squizzy Taylor was the Al Capone of Australia. We got a lot of publicity as a result. One of our concerns was that we always had a lot of female employees and this wasn't a safe district. Another tenant that moved in was the *'Maltese Mafia'*. We decided it would be a good step to make friends with them! We asked them to be the lookout for our girls to get safely out of the building and to their transportation at night. We were constantly thinking out of the box as I moved from a high-dollar established corporation to building one of our own.

In 1973, we had a Federal election and the Labour Party came into power for the first time in over twenty years. They were a militant "unionization" party. They wanted to nationalize key business areas and introduce a capital gains tax. Ogilvy & Mather, Leo Burnett and J. Walter Thompson all approached SPASM to buy us out. I also wanted to talk to Doyle Dane Bernbach (DDB). They were the number one creative advertising agency in the U.S. and probably the world at that time. When I was with Heinz in Pittsburgh, I'd worked with them when we developed Ketchup and Soup TV campaigns for the first time. These campaigns were very creative and original advertising and were highly effective in helping grow our market shares as part of the Heinz U.S. renaissance.

I called Bill Bernbach and told him that we were being approached by other U.S. ad agencies to consider selling. I asked if DDB might also be interested in talking to us. He told me Eddie Russell would come out the next week to meet with us (he was in charge of DDB International). After ten months of negotiating and a number of trips to New York City we ended up selling to them. We beat the time period before capital gains taxes were introduced in Australia. My partners and I stayed on with the new DDB in Australia with my role being management and operations and the other partners were involved in the creative side of the business. An immediate benefit for us was that DDB handled the Polaroid account around the world and they asked us to take that Polaroid advertising over for Australia.

After three years, DDB wanted me to come to the U.S. so that, on a global basis, I could manage the Polaroid International account from their worldwide headquarters in New York City. I moved to New York in January of 1978. Madge's two older children had just finished high school and they stayed back in Sydney. Our boys were eight and six; they had started grade school. As Madge was a U.S. citizen, the kids had joint citizenship. We lived in Chappaqua, New York and I commuted to New York City.

With accountability from January 1978 into 1981 for Polaroid's International advertising it took me all around the world; I traveled all over. Polaroid was one of the largest spending advertising clients in the U.S. at that time and they sold all over the world. A lot of the filming was in UK studios. Every once in awhile, there would be blowups between clients, directors and production set teams. I would take off from our office in NYC by helicopter, go over to JFK, and fly out to London on the Concorde to mediate and resolve conflicts. Hopefully, by the early hours in the morning, UK time, it would be resolved and I'd fly back to the U.S. by Concorde to be in my office by mid-morning – working on both sides of the Atlantic in one twenty-four-hour day!

I headed up the Polaroid account until 1981. At that time, we were assigned the Warner Communications account for Atari advertising to launch the video game industry into homes. I began flying weekly out to Silicon Valley where Atari was headquartered. I was always interested in what was going on in the world, particularly with technology, so that's how I tended to end up at the front of new waves.

The CEO of DDB was Neil Austrian. I would often stay at his home in Connecticut while visiting the U.S. when I still lived in Sydney. When DDB planned to bring me to New York, they sent me to the Harvard Business School for the Advanced Management Program in 1977. Neil was a Harvard MBA, loved sports and we got along very well.

Neil left DDB in mid-1984 to join Showtime as Chairman and CEO. Over the prior year he and I had been preparing for a major strategic presentation to the DDB Board about the next ten-year direction of the Company in a changing advertising environment. After Neil left, the new President of DDB had a very different personality and business profile to Neil; he had a fear of change, was much more comfortable in the known and did not support the forward looking strategy that I had been proposing.

Following right after Neil's departure from DDB I was being approached by a recruiting firm on behalf of a group of Venture Capitalists (Neil couldn't take me with him to Showtime because of his non-compete with DDB – however, he was the person who referred me to the Recruiting Firm). I accepted the position to join JH Whitney and Oak Management in one of their investments, Power.Base Systems . . . they were Blue Chip technology Venture Capitalists.

With the powerful self-awareness that came as a result of my psychological assessment in this recruiting process (Conceptual Advocate), I ended up getting the job as Senior VP of Marketing & Sales for Power.Base based in NYC. It was mid-1984. That's when desktop computers in the corporate world were just beginning. The CEO had created a database (Power.Base) that was a competitor to Dbase II (later Dbase III) owned by Ashton Tate. Our product was far superior; it was clearly "a better mousetrap". Dbase II/III was an earlier stage and simpler desktop database. Our product linked to mainframes, word documents, communication links, spreadsheets, graphics packages, etc. **Power.Base now needed the competitive marketing positioning.**

I took on that position to develop the marketing and sales strategy. As a member of the Board I was also exposed in the first month to the CEO's (the product inventor/developer) financial reporting, At the first monthly meeting I attended I didn't think the reported sales numbers made sense – the revenue didn't tie to anything that I could see in the sales reports. The second month, same thing...it didn't make sense.

I said to the CEO before our next Board meeting, "something's strange in the sales and financial reports and I want to discuss it with you."

Something didn't look right. The Founder/CEO owner was cooking the books. After I brought this issue with backup to the meeting, the Venture Capitalists (VCs) with Board control terminated the CEO and I was appointed the new CEO. This had not been my intent when I joined the company; however, reality needed to be addressed honestly.

The first thing I did was to understand the marketplace. We HAD the better mousetrap but a small market share at this time coming to market two years after Ashton Tate. Serious prospects were given twenty free trial samples. However, they were not buying on the follow up sales calls. I quickly identified the marketing issue: corporations at this early stage of desktop computers didn't have their own IT departments, training departments, technical support, etc. They loved Power.Base as a functional product, but they needed a support system that didn't exist at Power.Base in this new computer era. On the other hand, Ashton Tate did provide the necessary IT support *(it was a marketing problem and not a sales problem for Power.Base!).*

I needed to put together a business plan to deal with this discovery. The need wasn't the product; it was the 'Train the Trainer' and IT support. We had to create the infrastructure. Based on the Business Plan I put together, it would need a five million dollar investment to build the necessary infrastructure. The VC's who had already invested approximately ten million dollars to acquire and launch the product decided after three months of consideration not to make this additional investment. Instead, they asked me to work with an M&A firm to sell the business. We sold to Compuware in Detroit about a year later (an IBM mainframe and service company) because our product linked to mainframes and they could provide all the necessary IT support to their customers – it was an additional strategic product for their sales portfolio!

My business learning was very rapid given that I was unexpectedly CEO after only two months. First month after I became responsible to present the financial reporting, I typically presented the financials for the prior month and year-to-date. I was surprised when the VC's started to ask . ... . "no, not what happened but what WILL happen in the balance of the year? What are the repercussions of where we are at in the market place? What's the future financials going to look like by the end of the year?" During the second month I was still spending my time out in the field assessing the marketplace. At my second monthly Board meeting as CEO, same question. "We can read the financial report as well as you, but where's the business going to be at the end of the year?" Aha! FORECASTING! We all had budgets developed previously. However, the budgets were not real. That's when I created V-CAAR™.

This was an aha moment.

My determination of purpose and legacy may have been intentional, but whether I realized it or not, I was succeeding by default. I was being driven by that energy for work instilled by Paul Townsend and the love of work that led me through my early years in the business world. I was going, going, going, without effectively measuring or realizing the end point.

That's when I created V-CAAR™, an analytical AND action tool to forecast forward results (a PRESENT-FUTURE Mindset).

oooooooo

Today, the V-CAAR™ concept that was birthed in Boardrooms decades ago is the model I share with my own coaching clients (as well as the model that I use in my own professional and personal life). The V-CAAR™ process takes a look at financials and expenses, line by line to identify material variances in each line that exist when compared to what was expected (or planned) to happen in that review month period.

This is how I designed the V-CAAR™ process to work:

1. Identify the material **VARIANCES** line by line in the P&L Statement versus what was in the budget/forecast.
2. What was the **CAUSE** of the variance?
3. Now that we know the variance and the cause, what **ACTIONS** are we going to take for the rest of the year to deal with the situation. (Corrections for the balance of the year.)
4. Who is **ACCOUNTABLE** to execute the Actions?
5. **REFORECAST** the financials by month for the balance of the fiscal year based on the actions that will have financial ramifications.

That's the P&L…we also add, for each month, non P&L cash expense items (e.g. Capital expenses) and adjust for P&L non-cash items (e.g. Depreciation) so that the bottom line forecasts our Cash flow for each month (including Opening Cash and Closing cash balances).

With this V-CAAR™ tool, I have a financial, operations and cash flow tool to reforecast, each month, what the balance of the year should look like. I am also able to compare this year's full year P&L Reforecast to the full Prior-year and the full Original Budget as these are two other static columns in this model.

The questions that V-CAAR™ allows leaders to answer are:

Where will we be at the end of the year for our P&L and, importantly, where will we be for Cash flow based on updated reforecasts each month?

What monthly operating adjustments (reforecasts) need to occur NOW, this month?

What will our cash flow be like each forecast month for the remainder of the year?

Are we on-track toward purpose and legacy with regard to measurable results?

The V-CAAR™ is a living tool that develops throughout the year. If the company has already completed two of twelve months, the twelve months V-CAAR™ is two months of Actual and ten months of Reforecasts. When you add these twelve months to create Column thirteen, this is the new full year reforecast at this point in time. Column fourteen is the original Budget as static to compare with the now realistic monthly reforecast for the full year expected financial performance. I also include Column fifteen as the full reported prior year as an extra point of reference.

This V-CAAR™ tool formally requires

"I realized that the V-CAAR™ is a monthly analytical tool to measure results against any kind of planned expectation."

potential corrective action based on analysis to be taken every month to impact the full year performance proactively and not just "hope" the original budget is met. This is a PRESENT-FUTURE Mindset to successfully manage any business.

With my clients, we conduct V-CAAR™ every month to reforecast an expected full year financial and Cash flow performance.

In more recent coaching years, I have realized that V-CAAR™ is not a just financial tool, it's an ***analytical tool for any kind of expectations.*** Anytime there are milestones:

- o What are the VARIANCES?
- o What has CAUSED the variances?
- o What new ACTIONS are needed to impact positive future change?
- o Who is going to be ACCOUNTABLE to make the changes happen?
- o What will be the end RESULTS for the appropriate time the forecasted analysis is being made?

As one of my learning (and growing) experiences, I have now realized that the V-CAAR™ process can be applied ***TO ALL ASPECTS OF LIFE***: financial, sports, religious/spiritual, academic, political, medical, retirement plans, etc.

V-CAAR™ can be applied to any activity that can have metrics applied and appropriate timeframes for each of the activities. It is a process tool to manage/control actions and activities. It is based on the fundamental principle of a PRESENT-FUTURE Mindset to control future results and performance, not to just hope that results will occur.

"As one of my learning (and growing) experiences, I have now realized that the V-CAAR™ process can be applied TO ALL ASPECTS OF LIFE: financial, sports, religious/spiritual, academic, political, medical, retirement plans, etc."

~I.M.

	1	2	3	4	5	6
V-CAAR™ FINANCIAL	JAN	FEB	MAR	APR	MAY	JUN
	Actual	Actual	Actual	Actual	Actual	Actual
FROM PROFIT & LOSS (P&L):						
Gross Revenue	$					
Cost of Goods	$					
Gross Margin	$					
EXPENSES:						
Labor	$					
Labor Benefits	$					
Marketing	$					
Sales Expenses	$					
Rent and Facilities Expenses	$					
Utilities	$					
Travel	$					
Interest	$					
Taxes	$					
Depreciation	$					
Total Expenses	$					
NET INCOME (Gross Margin - Total Expenses)	$					
CASHFLOW ADJUSTMENTS:						
ADD: Non P&L Cash Receipts	$					
ADD: Month's Opening Cash	$					
ADD: P&L Non-Cash Expenses (eg. Depretiation)	$					
SUBTRACT: Capital Cash Expenses	$					
End of Month Cashflow FORECAST	$					

Concept model assumes six months Actual $ Results

CONCEPT MODEL*

7	8	9	10	11	12	13	14	15
JUL	AUG	SEP	OCT	NOV	DEC	TOTAL YEAR	ORIGINAL BUDGET	PRIOR YEAR
Reforecast	Reforecast	Reforecast	Reforecast	Reforecast	Reforecast	Reforecast	Current Year	Actual

and six months Reforecasted $ Results

Learn about setting goals in the Capital Region Business Journal article: *"Feeling Adrift? Write Down Your Goals"*(from December 2005). Additional Capital Region Business Journal articles, *"Test and Measure Again and Again"*(from July 2005), *"Play the Numbers Game to Reach Goals"* (from October 2006), and *"It's Not Just About the Numbers"* (from July 2006), help to address different aspects of the importance of forecasting results and can be found by scanning the below QR codes or visiting the correlating websites.

"Feeling Adrift? Write Down Your Goals"

https://goo.gl/3dBjJr

"Play the Numbers Game to Reach Goals"

https://goo.gl/NFuDi6

"Test and Measure Again and Again"

https://goo.gl/oefmKP

"It's Not Just About the Numbers"

https://goo.gl/w7UgIK

So You Can Analyze Your Journey, See Below:

<u>Consider a professional goal and its Time context that is not yet achieved:</u>

(It could be a financial goal, hiring goal, production goal, or any other critical area.)

V – What are the Variances between the goal and the achievement on a predetermined time period for analysis?

C – What could be key Causes of the variance?

A – What Actions should be taken now to track toward the original goal based on your period of analysis?

A – Who is in charge of the actions, who will be Accountable to make the planned changes happen?

R – Do you need to Reforecast the goal and how will the reforecast results compare to the original goal? How difficult will it be *culturally* to move into a PRESENT-FUTURE Mindset? *(Does the goal itself need to be adjusted positively or negatively, or perhaps the timeline of the goal needs modifying?)*

<u>Consider a personal goal that is not yet achieved:</u>

(It could be a weight loss goal, relationship goal, hobby goal, financial savings goal, or any other area in your life.)

V – What are the Variances between the goal and the achievement of the goal to-date?

C – What could be some of the Causes of the variance?

A – What Actions should be taken now to be on track toward the goal based on your analysis?

A – Who is Accountable for the actions to be taken?

R – Do you need to Reforecast the goal? *(Does the goal itself need to be adjusted positively or negatively, or perhaps the timeline of the goal needs modifying?)*

The Power of Disciplined
Time Management
. . . So You Can Make It Personal

"You may delay, but time will not."

~Benjamin Franklin, U.S. Founding Father

"Self-discipline is the key to personal greatness. With self-discipline, the average person can rise as far and as fast as his talents and intelligence can take him. But without self-discipline, a person with every blessing of background, education, and opportunity will seldom rise above mediocrity."

~Brian Tracy, Author and Motivational Speaker

*T*he power of Disciplined Time Management (DTM) is an extention and execution of a PRESENT-FUTURE Mindset. The V-CAAR™ is a tool used to track goals.The Disciplined Time Management tool will ensure that those goals are ones which are tracking from a two to three year strategic analysis all the way down to detailed plans on a daily basis. This tool is a method to keep on track toward, and aligned to, your Legacy.

In reviewing this tool, think about applying it to your professional path and separately think about it for your personal life. Also confirm that there is alignment in both paths to achieve specific "life" goals. And as this tool is for goal setting, whether it be for two years or for the next day, all goals need to be SMART goals. Specific Measurable Attainable Relevant Time-based.

DTM is the integration of Life and Business together to achieve the long term Legacy – it is an activity based planning tool. It requires knowing your Purpose, your WHY, so as to be able to create the future-picture vision of your Legacy. In other words, DTM represents the PRESENT-FUTURE Mindset for achieving goals with successful results.

As a coach, as an initial alignment meeting with a new client, I begin by asking about the lifetime achievements they desire, personal and professional. It is a big picture question that very few people put much thought into as most people are short term activity oriented and not big picture, strategic, future thinking oriented. This meeting should be held in a "comfort zone" location such as the person's home or in my office without distractions. If the business is a sole owner, it is appropriate to have the spouse participate in this business and personal alignment meeting – it is designed to get long term clarity before introducing DTM as an operating tool . . . questions such as:

What do you want to accomplish in your business life?

In your personal life?

What's your purpose . . . your WHY?

What do you want to leave behind as recognition as a lifelong achievements?

In regards to yoor your personal wealth?

What's a pragmatic vision for your future?

What do you want to be remembered for professionally?

Personally?

As a next step to start using DTM as a management operating tool and to stay on track toward the big picture, it is necessary to break the time line back down into small steps that are reasonably manageable in time segments as shown in the DTM model below:

Disciplined Time Management
A Backward-by-Design Personal Management Tool to Create Alignment in Life
A PRESENT-FUTURE Mindset Application by Iain Macfarlane

Strategic Plan – Two to Three Years Ahead

This is a reasonable first opportunity to become specific toward initial defined end results. At the two to three year level of planning, focus should be on strategic results. This is the first step in the annual Integrated Business Growth Process (IBGP) that has previously been discussed in The Power of the IBGP chapter.

Examples of Business questions:

- o *What is the target market category that you wish to operate in?*
- o *What market share do you want in that two to three year time period?*
- o *What financial size do you plan to be? Revenue? Net Profit?*
- o *What rate of growth makes sense as the Owner or top executive?*

Examples of Personal questions:

- o *What personal development and growth do I want to achieve?*
- o *What will be the key characteristics of relationships in my life?*
- o *What material achievements do I want to accomplish?*
- o *How do I want to achieve FUN in life?*

<u>*Operational Plan – One Year Ahead*</u>

These annual goals need to be operational and activity focused in nature. In reality, this Plan will be the **operating assumptions** to provide the basis for the Annual Budget and it is the second stage of the <u>**IBGP**</u>.

<u>*Examples of Business questions:*</u>

- o *What will be the budgeted financial performance results?* {This will require a review of the line by line P&L from prior year to finalize operating assumptions for each line item for the upcoming year budget.]
- o *What will be the most important operating drivers to provide those results?*
- o *What will be the marketing plan for the market positioning?*
- o *What organizational and staffing changes will be needed?*
- o *Based on Cashflow forecast, what additional funding will be needed?*

<u>*Examples of Personal questions:*</u>

- o *What personal income do I require?*
- o *What income including investment returns do I want to earn in the upcoming year?*
- o *What are my targeted improved relationship goals?*
- o *What specific educational growth needs will be beneficial?*
- o *What is my health plan for the upcoming year?*

As the one year Operational Plan is represented by the Annual Budget, managing performance against the Budget is through the V-CAAR™ process that is discussed in *The Power of the V-CAAR™* chapter.

<u>Results Planning – Ninety Days Ahead</u>

The most important period of time to measure and influence results against a full year performance expectation is the ninety days prior Quarter Review and the consequent upcoming Quarter refinement of targeted Results for that Quarter. This is the Results-Management/Reforecast stage of the *__IBGP__*.

A key exception to the importance of the Ninety Days RESULTS Planning most likely would be Retail operations where the Monthly Planning would be more important to adjust.

Experience has proven that humans can effectively absorb a detailed focus for ninety-day periods versus any longer time period. Consequently, there is a higher probability of achieving full year Annual Budget results because of human nature to focus on detailed Quarterly operations and the "feeling" of more control over a Quarter than a full year. And business success depends on people and individual performances as well as Team activities. And ninety days is an ideal time to review Team performance.

From one month planning (financial), down to one week planning (action), down to a single day of planning (schedule), you begin to work through the SMART Goal process (specific, measurable, achievable, realistic, time-bound goals). Manage the tasking of SMART Goals through a default calendar in which tasks are first prioritized and then time is assigned to those tasks according to need, putting "MUST DO" items in specific time blocks and other tasks into "open areas".

ooooooooo

The degree of difficulty of being disciplined at EACH stage of this DTM is in the reverse order; it is hardest for each individual day; the next hardest is for a week, then a month. When a day is finished, there is no going back to "make up" activities without the consequence of giving up something the next day. It is easier to find time to make up tasks, the longer the period available – it is easier in one week, than one day; it is easier to make up in one month than in one week, and so on.

Thus, the DAILY Discipline of Time Management is the most critical and usually the hardest to maintain!

The best way to document this process (DTM), beginning from daily through annual task management is to find a "Default Calendar" that each person is comfortable with, from old-fashioned hard-copy daily diaries to sophisticated digital tools. I'm still old-fashioned with the use of *The Original-Classic Franklin Covey Diary*. The choice of tool should be according to each person's comfort level; the key issue is that everyone should have their Disciplined Time Management process in place.

earn about disciplined time management in the specific Time Management articles, *"Quiz – Is your business killing you?"*, *"Positive attitude makes success an achievable goal"*, and *"Stop wasting time and get things done."* Scan the code at the right for your Disciplined Time Management learning.

"Quiz – Is Your Business Killing You?"

https://goo.gl/IWu3lP

"Positive Attitude Makes Success an Achievable Goal"

https://goo.gl/dzeOEb

"Stop Wasting Time and Get Things Done"

https://goo.gl/fl6TpO

Recap of Your Tools to Leave a Legacy

- o Integrated Business Growth Process (IBGP)
- o Vision and Strategy
- o Legacy
- o Purpose – WHY
- o Strategic Streamlining
  - o People
  - o Marketing
- o Operations to Achieve the Strategy
  - o Operational Roadmap
    - Create a Business Plan
      - o Get Outside Advice
      - o Analyze Historical Data
      - o Ask Pertinent Questions to Drive Toward Legacy
- o Routine Measures of Financial Results
  - o Get in the V-CAAR™
    - o Identify VARIANCES
    - o Identify CAUSES of variances
    - o Determine ACTIONS to take
    - o Assign ACCOUNTABILITY for actions
    - o REFORECAST future expectations
- o Influence and Inspiration of Staff to Drive Success
  - o Use Disciplined Time Management
    - o Maintain PRESENT-FUTURE Mindset
    - o Through routine check-ins at measured intervals, ensure tracking toward Legacy

"Disciplined Time Management is the integration of Life and Business together to achieve the long term Legacy."

~I.M.

The Power of Alignment

. . . So You Can Maximize Your Life

*"Try not to become a man of success but rather to
become a man of value."*

> *~Albert Einstein, Theoretical Physicist,
> Author, Philosopher*

From the time I began to think about the concept of Life Legacy, I became aware of the difference between what has often been called "life balance" and what I defined as "life alignment". The key difference is that life balance is a Past-Present Mindset where the results of spending time and effort to produce outcomes is based on assessing how life is being lived today and often reflects a satisfaction with current results. On the other hand, life alignment is a PRESENT-FUTURE Mindset assessing how satisfactions today are lining up to a picture of future results, to a future life style of expectations that will end up in an ongoing feeling of fulfillment. "Alignment" has been defined as an arrangement in correct or appropriate relative positions. This makes planning relative to an end result.

When I'm working with any person in any situation to help them improve their results or their performance, I begin by exploring WHY they are doing what they are doing? What results are they trying to achieve? Why is this so important? What has to be sacrificed to live this lifestyle? What are the consequences of not changing current habits? In many ways, I'm really challenging the person's comfort zone – most people I have this type of discussion, of every age, of every profession, of every educational background, find it difficult to challenge themselves on WHY they do what they do as this requires clarity in decision making that is something most people shy away from, potential life changing decisions.

My tool, or "formula", for Alignment is to check in with a person to be sure they know their WHY. *Where do you want to be in life over an extended period of an anticipated lifespan?* The approach of that one, simple question will:

- o DRIVE your Passion!
- o CREATE your Energy to EQUAL your Value!
- o Have the consequence of GENERATING your own:
    - o Influence
    - o Inspiration to:
        - o Impact others!

Alignment will not only change your own life, it will also change other people's lives and will make everyone more productive.

Early in my coaching career, I had an experience that had a big impact on my own understanding the difference between *life balance* (a practical existing lifestyle of owning a company, having a good income, a and finding time for family and friends and the things that are important) and *life alignment* (enthusiastic desire to go to work and come home feeling fulfilled every day). With an attitude of alignment, one wants to share the results of the day's work with family and friends and feel rewarded for every effort, both at work and at home. Value becomes an output rather than the cause of effort.

In my coaching, I was referred to a client by a sales consultant who recognized that growing this client's business was not a sales problem; it was a problem of the owner who didn't know why he was putting in so much effort for unsatisfactory results; it was a business problem coming from the owner's attitude and desire that impacted both employees and customers even though he, himself, felt he had a balanced life between business and home. He had family time as well as a good income and company.

Prior to getting married to his wife who had a very successful career in Investment Banking and who came from a wealthy family, this client had been a successful insurance sales person. That work was no longer needed; however, he felt he had to do something to support his *self-esteem* in his family environment.

His wife's family funded him to start his own company in promotional products to be sold into corporations as promotional awards to successful employees. As an experienced salesperson, he did very well in gaining clients for his business . . . his sales grew! He felt he needed to keep selling more and growing quickly to represent to his family how well he was doing. He achieved sales of five million dollars in less than five years of business. What he didn't see, though, is that – while his sales were high – his expenses were even higher.

Not understanding the financial elements of building a business, my client had continued working harder without realizing the business was losing significant money – he was equating his visible hard work efforts, as seen by his family, to being successful in business. In reality, his family was funding his losses and didn't want to upset his image by raising that as an issue. As he realized that his sales results didn't seem to be producing profits, he became distressed and emotionally bankrupt in his personal and professional relationships.

When I started working with him, I immediately held an Alignment with him in a meeting that took more than six hours. We met in his home where my goal was to make him as comfortable as possible to really understand his WHY.

I asked him many questions to help him start to realize the impact of his own answers. Why do you own this business? Do you like it? What benefit are you enjoying from the success? What did you love about work in the past? What was your purpose in that work? What is your purpose in this work? On and on our session went, digging down layer by layer until we got to the heart of what work mattered to him; we also visualized a future picture (PRESENT-FUTURE Mindset, of course)!

It turned out that what my client really wanted to do was to be an executive for a *non-profit* organization. His goal was to help under privileged children.

On understanding the power of what this purpose could do, he was able to create value in his work. Vision and motivation drove his next efforts. He embraced his goal of helping to improve other's lives. In his new role, he was providing real value to others and, just as importantly, to himself. This client was not driven by money to prove his worth to his family. He wanted to work, but toward a personal purpose . . . a personal WHY.

I helped him sell his company and now, eight years later, he has an exciting career as a senior executive in a non-profit supporting disadvantaged children. This career has aligned his work life and his family life. He is emotionally committed to his purpose in life.

What is your WHY?

Life's experiences, the lessons gained from them, and the tools to guide those lessons, mean nothing if you don't know what you are being guided toward. That's what the power of alignment is all about.

So you can discover your WHY, ask yourself questions such as:

1. What drives you?
2. What makes you laugh?
3. What makes you cry?
4. What excites you to work harder . . . not to notice time passing?
5. What gives you the greatest enjoyment while at home?
6. What social activities do you most enjoy?
7. What kind of books do you want to read a second time?
8. What activities make you relax the most emotionally and physically?

"Life's experiences, the lessons gained from them, and the tools to guide those lessons, mean nothing if you don't know what you are being guided toward."

~I.M.

Marriage has been the greatest adventure of all. Here,
Madge and Iain, on their wedding night, phone Iain's
parents in Australia to share the exciting news,
September 24th, 1966

Part 4
Legacy is Not a
One-Person Endeavor

"That day in Mexico changed my life forever . . . although, I didn't know it at the time . . ."

~I.M.

The Power of Living and

Leaving A Legacy

. . . So You Can Remember

Why You Began

"The best time to plant a tree was twenty years ago.

The second best time is now.

~Chinese Proverb

As part of my East-West Center Fellowship, I was required to do a research project in the summer of 1963 and then attend the Fall 1963 semester on the U.S. Mainland. (I was accepted for the Fall semester into the Graduate Business School at Columbia University in New York.) The travelling research project I chose was *"The application of computers in the American Steel Industry"* as I had anticipated at this time that I would return to Australia after the EWC to work for Broken Hill Proprietary (BHP); they had given me a two year leave-of-absence to attend the EWC.

I pre-arranged interviews with steel companies across the United States, beginning in the west and ending up in New York City in time to start at Columbia. I had purchased a

Continental Trailways $99 ticket that allowed me to travel anywhere for up to ninety-nine days. I initially flew from Honolulu to Denver for my first interview. From there I headed west through Salt Lake City where I was hosted by a woman who put me up in her home for two nights. She was the mother of George Romney and the grandmother of Mitt Romney. Apart from my research interview, she showed me Salt Lake City, including a visit to hear the Mormon Tabernacle Choir. I continued onto San Francisco, Los Angeles, Las Vegas, and the Hoover Dam, before making my way to Phoenix, Arizona. After Phoenix, my next interview was in Houston and I had a week to get there. I was a free man for seven days!

I realized I could get down to Mexico City and see it as long as I flew back to Houston. Starting in Nogales, I took local buses all the way to Mexico City (sleeping in those buses while travelling overnight). I got to Mexico City after four days and had the following day and evening in Mexico City before my flight to Houston.

I ended up with 'Montezuma's Revenge' by the time I got to Mexico City. It was my punishment for indulging local foods over the past several days. As I'd come so far and really wanted to see Mexico City I needed to come up with a solution to my predicament! I decided to splurge on a one-day limo trip. The driver would pull over if I needed a quick exit.

There were five of us in the car: two women from New York, me, and a young, beautiful woman from Detroit on her vacation, along with her mother. The Michigan native was named Madge. That day in Mexico City changed my life forever...although I didn't know it at the time. After three more years of education and learning about life, this one day meeting in Mexico City led to a fifty-year marriage that began on September 24, 1966, and proved that *"the power of living"* and creating a lifelong legacy is not a one person endeavor.

On that trip to Mexico, I was still a young, "idealistic international". I started talking about American problems, particularly as this was the summer of Civil Rights in the U.S. Madge and I got into a number of...heated discussions...let's call them debates. When the tour took us to a Cathedral that was beautiful and rich in gold—but also surrounded by poor beggars—we had even more discussions. These ones had us on the same page.

At the end of the day-trip, Madge's mother said, "What are you doing for dinner?" I said I'd figure something out; her mother invited me to join them. At the end of dinner, her mother said to me, "If you're ever near Detroit, stop by". She didn't realize that when you say that to an Australian, they think you really mean it.

ooooooooo

It was July now. I flew to Houston, then by bus again to Dallas. Then, I moved into the Deep South: New Orleans, Louisiana, Jackson, Mississippi, and Birmingham, Alabama.

When I got on the Continental Trailways bus in Jackson, I sat down in the back of the bus. The driver said, "Before I leave here, sonny, you'd better come sit up front or I won't begin driving." I wonder what Madge would have said were she there. Two days later, I left Birmingham for Atlanta a short while before Governor George Wallace turned the dogs on the people. From Atlanta, I went to on to Chattanooga. I was still relatively naïve. I wasn't fearful because I didn't have the depth of understanding of what was going on in the societal revolution of 1963. I didn't know what was behind the whole story. I went to Memphis, where the only place to keep cool enough to sleep was a local all-night movie theater. Then, I went onto St. Louis, along the Mississippi River.

From St. Louis, I went to Chicago and stayed with a professor and his wife on the South Side. The first day, they told me where to catch a bus to get to Downtown Chicago. I walked the two blocks and turned right walking to the corner where I had to catch the bus. There was a fight on the corner between white and black groups of young males. I turned around immediately and went back to the house I had come from. I learned later that day on the news that two of the black boys had been murdered. I now realized what was going on in this violent Civil Rights summer.

I continued onto Gary, then Toledo . . .

. . . with a stop in Detroit on the way to meet up with Madge and her mother! They did say, "if you're ever near Detroit . . . ." My stop turned into a day, and then two, before I was forced to move onto Toledo.

From Toledo . . . to Cleveland . . . to Pittsburgh, THE STEEL CITY . . . to Syracuse. It was only September by this time, but I saw my first snow, there.

I had never consciously thought of snow as wet. I never realized it. It was logical, of course, but I'd only ever seen it in movies and I'd simply thought of it as soft and fluffy!

"*I had never consciously thought of snow as wet. It was logical, of course, but I'd only ever seen it in movies and I'd simply thought of it as white and fluffy.*"

Travels Through the United States and Mexico (West)

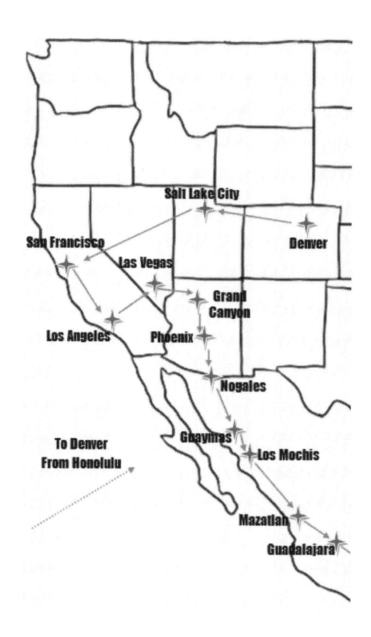

Travels Through the United States and Mexico (East)

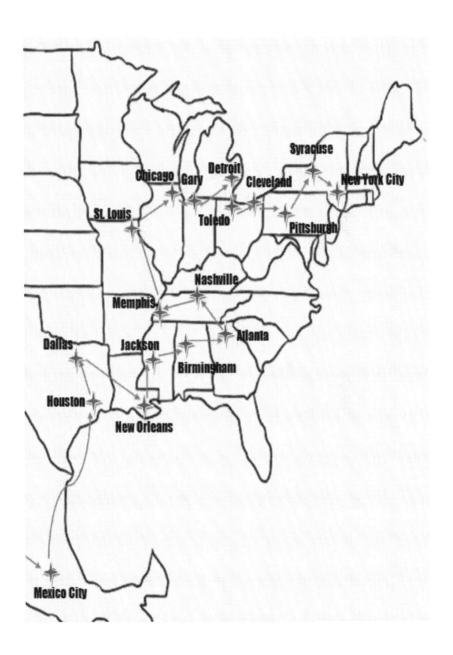

ooooooooo

In New York State is where my summer-long bus journey completed.

While in Syracuse, I stayed with a friend of mine who I got to know at the University of Hawaii while I was at the East-West Center. As he was also planning to attend Columbia, we decided to share an apartment. As the semester came upon us, we drove to our rental apartment in Spanish Harlem at West 153rd Street just off Broadway and with a view of the George Washington Bridge and the Hudson River.

I immediately went down into the city taking a subway and came up at 42nd Street in Times Square. At street level all I could see were buildings that went into the sky all around me. I had to get to 39th and 3rd. In Australia, you just go up to any policeman and ask for directions. I went up and said, "Excuse me, could you tell me how to get to 39th and 3rd." He said, "Sonny, if you don't know how to do that, you don't belong in this city." It was my *New York Welcome*.

I decided to make the most of my semester in NYC. It cost just ten cents for the subway and it was relatively safe at that time. I had no fear on the subway, even on my own and at any time of day or night when coming home from late night parties. Also, the United Nations was right there. If there was a national leader presenting, I would go and listen to their keynote addresses.

I saw the Jets, the Yankees, art Galleries, and Broadway! If I'd done a good day's work at Columbia, I'd get a seat in the back rows for $2.50 (***I learned The Power of Reward***). Lincoln

Center had just recently opened and the conductor was Leonard Bernstein. Seats to see him ran me about $2.00!

The Summer and Fall semesters of 1963 were as much impactful times for this Australian to live as they were for any American: civil rights, Kennedy killed, and the freedom to appreciate the greatness and some of the downsides of what America offered were overwhelming experiences. I was able to learn and personally grow.

During that Fall semester, Madge and her mother invited me to join them in Detroit for Christmas. (Apparently, they hadn't learned their lesson! I stayed with them until the day before New Year's Eve!)

Back in buses for the round trip, I returned to New York in time for the New Year's Eve celebration in Times Square – even in 1963 there were a million people packed in Times Square to watch the ball fall at midnight.

I returned to the East-West Center in Honolulu in February to finish my final semester and to graduate with my MBA Degree.

At that Christmas break in Detroit there was no serious commitment from either Madge or myself - she was also completing her Master's degree at Michigan State University in Psychiatric Social Work specializing in battered children, and raising two little children as a single mother.

Even though the Legacy really began in the Summer of 1963, in Mexico City, the real beginning of our Legacy as a joint endeavor didn't begin until after I returned to the U.S. (in Pittsburgh) in 1965, to begin my business career at the Heinz Company. It was now a year and a half since Mexico and it was a year after I'd last seen her when I visited them for Christmas (Madge, Ruth, Madge's step dad, and Madge's two children, Doug and Den who were seven and five at that time).

Now planning to be in one place for awhile, I bought a 1965 Mustang Fastback as soon as I arrived in Pittsburgh – it was the first one ever delivered into Pennsylvania! On my return to the States, I cold called Madge and blatantly asked whether she was now married or committed. When I called, part of my intent was to test drive my new car from Pittsburgh to Michigan.

A year after I had last seen Madge or even communicated with her, I was still thinking of her. A year later!

I drove from Pittsburgh once or twice a month (in those days, traffic was a lot lighter and high speeds were not policed like they are today). I had to balance these trips with my role in the renaissance of Heinz . . . it was a staff of bright, young, energetic people putting in early mornings, late nights, and many weekends. After a few months, Madge also made an occasional trip to Pittsburgh.

I knew that I would be going back to Australia at the end of 1966 as part of my agreement with Heinz.

In March of 1966 I proposed.

My proposal was really the first hindsight realization that we would have to make a huge decision, particularly Madge; I was essentially asking her to move her KIDS to another COUNTRY. Who does that? Who would embrace such risk?

Madge had done an incredible job of raising them, and motivating, and teaching, and educating, so she did the biggest job in explaining what a move to Australia would look like. In reality, we had to both have a PRESENT-FUTURE Mindset.

We were married in Birmingham Michigan on September 24, 1966 and my brother Alan came from his college in California to be my Best Man. Madge and the two boys moved to Pittsburgh a week after our honeymoon in Upper Peninsula Michigan. It was a small two bedroom apartment and perfect for me and my new bride.

oooooooo

We decided when we went back to Australia in December, to make it an extended Europe-Asia trip. We started in London staying in the Heinz Family luxury apartment in the Grosvenor House including a driver and car (this was also Princess Margaret's car and driver when she was in London). Great experiences. We then went to Paris for a couple of days around Madge's interest in art. She loved art and was knowledgeable but was not yet an experienced painter herself – that came later as part of her legacy. From Paris, we went to Vienna and bought artifacts and specifically a beautiful Russian religious icon. Then, West Berlin to Checkpoint Charlie through to East Berlin on our way to Moscow. On a small bus as we left West Berlin into East Berlin, there was a warning sign that you were leaving U.S. protection (and this was at the height of the Cold War!). U.S. Military entered and gave a final verbal warning; then the East German military came on the bus and took all of our passports; twenty minutes later they came back and handed back all but one of the passports. A young, American boy was taken off the bus and it was the last we knew of him.

Two days after we arrived in Moscow, a huge blizzard hit. On this trip, we were flying British Airways (BOAC) from

Moscow to Delhi. In those days, the airline was responsible if they couldn't fly you, so they had to put up my family. We stayed at the Hotel Peking in Moscow. It had been donated by China to the Soviets. It's where diplomats would stay. We had previously been told by the travel agent that every room was bugged; so we taught the children not to speak anything disparaging.

Madge took the two boys down to breakfast after the second morning with a blizzard whiteout now going on. An Indian man and young woman were at the next table at breakfast. He offered to take us around Moscow with his interpreter as soon as conditions allowed.

This gentleman was Dr. Mulk Raj Annand, an internationally known writer for his works on the poor in India; I had great conversations with him about my trip through India in 1964. He was a guest of the Soviet Government. He and his interpreter, Tanya, took us to Lenin's Tomb, right to the front of a line that stretched more than a mile around Red Square. They also took us to the Bolshoi Ballet to see Swan Lake. One other memorable experience was that he took us to a truly exclusive private club called The Union primarily for the highest level of Government officials. . . . to this day the best Chicken Kiev I've had anywhere in the world. It was late at night, and in came a huge entourage. The head of the entourage stopped, and then leapt into a bear hug with Dr. Annand. The two had studied together in Paris. The Soviet who was one of five members of the Presidium Council asked for us to join his table and the vodka started flowing. We had more and more food until the early hours in the morning . . . WITH the two kids. At the end of our late dinner, the Russian said, "I want to propose a toast that the children of your children will meet with my grandchildren on the moon in peace." WOW, what an experience!

Dr. Annand side note – he knew Picasso in Paris. Government officials had recently discovered some of Picasso's art, commissioned by Russian Royalty in Moscow prior to the 1917 Revolution, and were paintings that had never been released to or seen by the public at this time. We got to see these paintings in a private showing because of Dr. Annand's relationship with the Soviet Government! The work had been discovered buried under a castle since the revolution.

We flew to Delhi . . . after having spent ten days in Moscow . . . and then onto Bangkok. We stayed with the daughter of my mother's headmaster from her Phuket teaching days in the mid-1930s. Then onto Singapore, and finally to Sydney.

ooooooooo

After this Europe and Northern Asia excursion, formally having covered most of the world, we arrived in Australia a week ahead of Christmas and spent the holiday at my family home in Sydney with my parents. From there, it was onto Melbourne to begin my Heinz Melbourne career.

Just the fact that Madge made this commitment, going into the unknown, going through East Berlin and Moscow as an American during the height of the Cold War, reflects that we both had (have) an element of adventure and a belief that we can handle ourselves in any circumstance. Doing exciting things is part of our lives. Perhaps, even subconsciously, we are always looking for excitement.

This became part of our legacy together.

> **"**Just the fact that Madge made this commitment, going into the unknown, going through East Berlin and Moscow as an American during the height of the Cold War, reflects that we both had (have) an element of adventure and a belief that we can handle ourselves in any circumstance. **"**

ooooooooo

In Melbourne, the Heinz factory and office was about twenty miles outside of the main city. The company had rented a house for us to allow us time to get acclimated and decide in what area we wanted to live. Our goal was to find a house to buy even though we had almost no money at that time. We did have some furniture from Madge's home and my 1964 Mustang that we shipped from the U.S. (my car had to be converted to right seat driving within six months of our arriving in Australia).

We found a small house on Port Phillip Bay, twenty-two miles from the Heinz office and across primarily farm country. The house was a small 'weekender' owned by a leading Melbourne and well known surgeon. The asking price was $15,000. Two bedrooms, brick, on a nice bit of land that looked out over Port Phillip Bay. I was able to get the Managing Director of Heinz to talk to the bank so that I could get a $10,000 mortgage. I asked the Real Estate agent to talk to the owner. I called to talk to him on the phone and asked if I could please come visit him to talk about how I could buy his house. He was well known to be an arrogant unapproachable person by nature. I went with the whole family to meet him at his Melbourne home. I asked if he'd fund the $5,000 balance that I would pay off over five years. He wasn't letting down his guard. Dr, Hamley Wilson's wife said, "I want you to do it." He did. I paid it off in three years. It was a spectacular location in Mt Eliza overlooking Port Phillip Bay and felt even better having negotiated a 100% financing including a deal with Dr. Wilson who I had been told was unapproachable.

oooooooo

Coming back to Madge, here she was in a foreign country in this little weekender home, nothing familiar to the normal household and shopping amenities she had been used to. Most of what she'd been used to in America didn't even exist in Australia at that time. There was no heating except for a little fireplace. She had to become part of a new school system for the two boys. Being a very successful person herself, going through all these changes . . . and she never threw her arms up!

She became President of the Mother's Association. We befriended Phillip and Leah Lynch who had two boys the same age as ours. That year, Phillip was elected to the Australian Parliament and we quickly surrounded ourselves with people we enjoyed and who had similar interests to ourselves.

Madge decided not to work as we were living out in the "boonies" in what was primarily a summer vacation area and making a new life in a new country was really a full time job anyway. She started exploring her passions around art and cooking (with a lot of new Australian ingredients to play with). Initially, she tried pottery as an art medium. After pottery, she moved onto oils. Rob was born in 1969 and, two years later, Jeff was born in 1971.

When Madge went into labor with Jeff, I called our doctor who said go to the hospital where he would meet us in thirty to forty minutes. The Mornington Bush Hospital was fifteen minutes away with no doctor in attendance and only one nurse. I pulled up in front and the nurse and I got Madge into a room. Before the doctor came, I DELIVERED JEFF with the nurse. The doctor arrived, said, "Good job!" and was off again.

The birth of any child is as high as any experience emotionally that a parent can go through. Just to bring life into being is the greatest honor.

Madge adapted quickly although it may not have seemed like that at the time. (We did put in a heating system because it does get cold at night on the Bay in Melbourne!) Perhaps it was Madge's earlier professional career before we were married that prepared her for the challenges of creating a new life for a growing family in a foreign environment. She was educated in and technically trained in psychiatric social work specializing in battered children, not just anywhere but in the inner heart of the worst of Detroit. She was instrumental in writing the first legislation for the State of Michigan and this became a blueprint for Federal legislation. Every day was an emotional day. But she believed in what she was doing, she was willing to put herself out every day and she was willing to put herself at risk to do it. She always challenged herself then, and ever since, to go to another level. Her mindset was always to be skilled, to be accomplished and to always do better at every challenge she took on. Perhaps after that, I was not such a difficult challenge!

We have both always had a travel bug: to go to exciting places, to reflect on different cultures, on different ages of history, and to do exciting things when we're travelling. On the trips we were taking to Mexico in 1963 when we met in Mexico City, after I had left to fly to Houston, she went scuba diving and open-water fishing in Acapulco. She ended after a number of hours of hauling in a 'big' fish, it turned out to be a ten-foot, six-inch long sailfish that was, then, a world record for a woman!

After we were settled back in the U.S. in 1978 and I had to do a lot of worldwide travel in my role with Polaroid International, she made many trips with me . . . and it was her presence that always made the trip more enjoyable.

oooooooo

As soon as we moved to Melbourne, we used to love going to art galleries. There was one at the top of our street and we saw a painting by Pro Hart that we really liked. It was one of his early paintings. He was a silver miner in Broken Hill. And he'd use building paints to start painting. This was one of his earlier paintings on masonite. It was $2,000.00. We didn't have the money and we realized we needed a new refrigerator. We spoke to the owner of the Manyung Gallery who had recognized our love for the painting. He asked how he could help us. He said, "what if you let it hang here. You bought it. And you pay what you can until you've paid it off." It took around a year.

ooooooo

In hindsight, an unbelievable contribution that Madge made to our life together was the fact that, while I was driving my new primary career at Heinz, at the same time I took on teaching Undergraduate and Graduate courses after normal work hours for two years at Monash University, and I also had a small management consulting job, Madge was supportive. She was, without question, running the home show. She became a master cook and gardener! What we each did was appreciated. We each respected that the other had individual passions that needed outlets and shared responsibilities that needed recognition.

We shared work around the house and yard and kept a social life with other couples and families in our neighborhood. We shared reading and art. Wherever we've moved in our fifty years together, particularly as Madge became more involved in painting - watercolors since we came back to the U.S. in 1978 - we've shared activities together.

Madge has always been involved in everything I do in business, not just my past thirteen years of business coaching, but also during my corporate executive level work. We always hosted clients and employees in our home. We always interacted with staff. Madge can naturally handle people better than I can. She enjoys people and relationships intellectually and socially; she's adaptable. I never have to worry in any environment.

Madge and I are both strong enough individually that her self-confidence allows her to meet people easily. She's very sensible and can read people. She wants to help people in circumstances that they need help in. She didn't apply her psychological studies medically as a career, but she certainly did in personal relationships. She's highly intelligent.

ooooooooo

Even though our interests are in different areas, we share conversations that the other wants to hear about. She was not active in sports, although she did do baton twirling at some Detroit Lions games and we have played golf together frequently for many years until she suffered a back injury a few years ago. When we moved back to the U.S. in January 1978, we lived in Chappaqua (New York). Having just moved back to the States, we joined Whippoorwill Country Club because I knew I would have a lot of international travel and that a country club would be a good centering point for Madge and the kids. The Club was less than two miles away. We were able to meet socially with other business people and community leaders. Madge took up golf and became quite good and became President of the Ladies' Club. This would provide involvement, connections, and friendships at the highest levels knowing that Madge would be taken care of while I was travelling on extended trips.

Leadership as a legacy.

Leadership is influence.

Madge has a strong influence with all the people she comes in contact with . . . most of all . . . *me.*

We've always had a shared leadership mindset. Pittsburgh. Melbourne. Chappaqua. Knoxville. Minneapolis. Madison.

We jointly made home decisions; then she took over the home. To the extent it involved me, whether I had a different point of view or not, I was always comfortable with her decisions. I was happy and appreciative of the way we worked things out. There is a total trust that I have with Madge. Each of us is fully supportive of the other's achievements, offering encouragement and adding value without blocking. We respect one another and never question it unless we feel we can take the thoughts to another level.

ooooooooo

Love is the greatest legacy of all and I discovered mine in the middle of Montezuma's Revenge. It is love that strengthens me for the message of the tombstone. It allows me to be involved, to inspire, and to influence others toward their WHYs. Madge doesn't just help me make the legacy . . . she IS the legacy. How honored I am to be her husband.

What is your greatest legacy?

Above – on the same Mexico trip on which she met Iain, Madge stands with her catch, a 10-Foot, 6-Inch Sailfish which, at the time, stood as the world record for women!

Below – on their honeymoon in Mackinac Island, Michigan, Iain looks onto his two most prized loves . . . Madge and his Ford Mustang.

*Above — Madge's art studio in the Madison
home where she and Iain live.*

*Below — Art storage for Madge's many
watercolors and other award-winning artwork.*

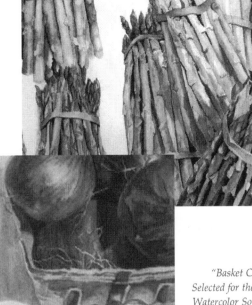

"Asparagus"

Second Place in Watercolor

Hilton Head Art League

"Basket Cases" Selected for the National Watercolor Society 90th International Exhibition 2015

Madge today. See more of her art at: Madgemacfarlanestudio.com Or scan the QR code!

Legacy is Not a One-Person Endeavor

Leftt – Madge and Iain with their first Great Granddaughter
Center Left – Iain and Madge's son, Jeff, in Saddam Hussein's palace after the fall of Baghdad, Iraq during the Iraq War
Center Right – Madge and Iain's son, Den, lost a courageous battle to cancer, but he still lives on as part of his family's memories
Bottom – On the occasion of their fiftieth anniversary, four generations of the Macfarlane family celebrate the love and legacy that Iain and Madge began all those years before

The Power of a Lifetime

. . . So You Can Begin with the

End in Mind

"Your true legacy is the outcome of your life's experiences."

~Iain Macfarlane

*O*ne of the most common environments I see when working with businesses is that if there are issues limiting achievement of planned results, it usually boils down to some element of lack of trust within the team. Trust requires total commitment and total commitment requires trust. Teamwork comes from that mutual commitment. Always search for ways that trust can be reflected in an unconditional way; to the extent that it's recognized when trust is missing, find ways to deal with it. Without trust, you can't succeed . . . and nobody can succeed alone.

In a relationship which goes forever, it's a matter of putting the effort into understanding the passions and needs of the other party and to find ways that your own passions have evolved in a way that creates common interest. You don't have to have the same passions; it's how you use different passions to create common interests. A positive concern for respect, sharing, giving to the other where they are at, and truly enjoying the activity . . . enjoying the fact that you are giving as well as receiving.

ooooooo

Legacy is the outcome of your life's experiences.

When I'm getting to know somebody professionally, I do a personal alignment upfront through a four-hour interview to get to understand them. As a last question, I ask them what they want on their tombstones. Why and what outcomes are they looking for from coaching? What is their purpose for being in the business that they are in; what is their WHY? It's necessary for there to be an alignment between the person and their "purpose" goals and between the person and their coach. Then I can support people to work towards their own legacy.

Legacy in professional life or in personal life is not a one-person endeavor and it will be stronger, and better, and more exciting, and more fulfilling as it is shared over time with someone else to whom you can be close and with whom you can share mutual passions.

As I learned and continuously grew . . . a process that is unending . . . through a wide range of experiences, that influenced the person I became, my legacy goals evolved and eventually became very clear to me. I live with the comfort of knowing the tombstone words toward which I've worked.

That's The Power of I Am . . . So I Can!

Iain Macfarlane

He helped others get results they otherwise would not have achieved without his Involvement, Influence, and Inspiration.

So You Can Remember Why You Began, Journal Below:

Why have you begun your journey?

_____

_____

_____

What is it that you can plan to achieve through this journey?

_____

_____

_____

Write your most powerful personal goal.

_____

_____

_____

Write your most powerful professional goal.

_____

_____

_____

What words are you working toward for your tombstone?

_____

_____

_____

What is your biggest takeaway from "The Power of I Am?"

_____

_____

_____

_____

_____

_____

_____

_____

_____

_____

_____

_____

_____

_____

Part 5
Powerful
Resources

"Your true legacy is the outcome

of your life's experiences."

~I.M.

Powerful Reads - "The Power of I Am ... So I Can"

Personal:

The Scottish Radicals, Tried and Transported to Australia for Treason in 1820 – Margaret and Alastair Macfarlane

John Watts, Australia's Forgotten Architect 1814-1819 and South Australia's Postmaster General 1841-1861 – Margaret and Alastair Macfarlane

The Crimes of Patriots (A True Tale of Dope, Dirty Money, and the CIA) – Jonathan Kwitny

Gems from IDRIESS – Ion Idriess

Leadership:

The Maxwell Daily Reader – John C. Maxwell

5 Levels of Leadership – John C. Maxwell

21 Irrefutable Laws of Leadership – John C. Maxwell

GOOD LEADERS Ask GREAT Questions – John C. Maxwell

EVERYONE COMMUNICATES FEW CONNECT – John C. Maxwell

8 Lessons In Military Leadership for Entrepreneurs – Robert T. Kiyosaki

The 7 Secrets of Exceptional LEADERSHIP – Brian Tracy

The Little Book with 50 BIG Ideas on LEADERSHIP - Glenn Furuya

Motivation

Oh, the Places You'll Go! – Dr. Suess

MIND GYM (An athlete's guide to inner excellence) – Gary Mack with David Casstevens

Awaken the Giant Within – Anthony Robbins

Drive (The Surprising Truth About What Motivates Us) – Daniel H. Pink

Secrets of the Obvious (A guide for balanced living) – Harry Cohen

Personal Development

Start with WHY - Simon Sinek

The 7 Habits of Highly Effective People – Stephen R. Covey

Good To GREAT -Jim Collins

The Success Principles (How to get from where you are to where you want to be) - Jack Canfield

THINK AND GROW RICH (Your Key to Financial Wealth and Power) - Napoleon Hill

The Power of ATTITUDE - Mac Anderson

Little Gold Book of YES! Attitude (How to find, build, and keep a YES! Attitude for a Lifetime of Success) - Jeffrey Gitomer

Eat That Frog! *(21 great ways to stop procrastinating and get more done in less time)* – Brian Tracy

The COMPOUND EFFECT - Darren Hardy

Rich Dad, Poor Dad – Robert T. Kiyosaki& Sharon L. Lechter

Stress is a Choice (10 Rules to Simplify your Life) – David Zerfoss

How to Win Friends & Influence People – Dale Carnegie

SELF-RELIANCE (The Wisdom of Ralph Waldo Emerson as Inspiration for Daily Living) – Richard Whelan

Day by Day with James Allen -Vic Johnson

The Secrets of Writing Letters That Really Work… WRITE LANGUAGE – Allan Pease and & Paul Dunn

NETWORKING Like a Pro (Turning Contacts into Connections) – Ivan Misner, David Alexander, & Brian Hilliard

Team Development

The Advantage (Why Organizational Health Trumps Everything Else in Business) – Patrick Lencioni

The Five Dysfunctions of a Team – Patrick Lencioni

Business Development

The Instant Success Series – Bradley J. Sugars (ActionCOACH Business Coaching)

The E Myth Revisited (Why most small businesses don't work and what to do about it) – Michael E. Gerber

Sales Bible – Jeffrey Gitomer

Uplifting Service (The Proven Path to Delighting Your Customers, Colleagues, and Everyone Else You Meet) – Ron Kaufman

AMAZE Every Customer Every Time – Shep Hyken

The Third Wave – Steve Case

Management

The One Minute Manager – Ken Blanchard & Spencer Johnson

TIME MANAGEMENT – Brian Tracy

Who Moved My Cheese? (An Amazing way to deal with Change in your work and in your life) – Spencer Johnson & Ken Blanchard

Secrets *of the World Class(Turning Mediocrity into Greatness)*-Steve Siebold

Blue Ocean Strategy (How to create uncontested market space and make the competition irrelevant) – W. Chan Kim & Renee' Mauborgne

Mastering the Rockefeller Habits – Verne Harnish

The ESSENTIAL DRUCKER – Peter F. Drucker

The Absolutely Critical Non-Essentials – Dr. Paddi Lund

Building the Happiness-Centered Business – Dr. Paddi Lund

EmPOWERing You!

Powerful Articles

Download nearly fifty practical articles for running your business in a manner that connects personal purpose with professional success. "Powerful Articles for Business Leaders" is available on Kindle for just $7.99. Purchase at https://goo.gl/ym8ELZ or scan the code at the right.

Powerful Business Journal

Purchase a professional journal filled with additional inspirational quotes, as well as additional copies of the tools to build a legacy, and journaling and goal setting sections. Continue to check the Electronic Resource Hub for updates on the Business Journal!

Electronic Resource Hub

Don't forget that you can check out the online resource page where there is additional information from "The Power of I Am . . . So I Can" in addition to contact forms, great photos, and more!

"WHY have you started this journey?

What will your tombstone say?"

~I.M.

ACKNOWLEDGMENTS

My inspiration to consider writing a book came from my parents who wrote two historical books on our family so their offspring would have a better understanding and appreciation of where we came from and, perhaps, a better understanding of who we are. I began my path to follow their lead eighteen months ago.

I extend my sincere appreciation to the publishing team of Reji Laberje Writing and Publishing led by Reji Laberje who—over many meetings and countless hours of collaborating—was my guide, contributing writer, interior designer, process manager, and publishing team leader. It was easy to *think* about writing a book...and difficult to commit to it. After discussions with Reji, it became easy to commit to the project knowing the support she and her team were going to provide.

I extend my gratitude to members of Reji's team who provided the integrated pieces to suddenly allow the book to appear as an achievement: RaeAnne Marie Scargall, the editor who had the task of working with my Aussie/American writing style; Michael Nicloy who worked with me on the cover design using my favorite personal photo as a fixed decision; Kimberly Laberge who supplemented my photos with her photography and map drawings for both the book and the complementary Electronic Resource Hub, and Angela Nicloy who partnered with my own marketing professional to make sure that this book ended up in the hands of those who it could help as they work toward their own legacies. On my own end, I must also offer my sincere appreciation to MaryLee Engelke, my part-time office manager and marketer, who survived my old-fashioned dictation of a LOT of copy.

Also, for so many people who have influenced my life and helped me to become the person *I AM*, from teachers and educators, to sports partners and competitors, and to the wide range of professional and personal friends I have had contact with across the world over more than seven decades, I am truly thankful. In particular, I owe so much to the business mentors in my employee and employer roles, as well as to my many business clients over the past thirteen years, who have all influenced and taught me as we worked together in professional and coaching relationships.

During the coaching era of my business life, I specifically want to thank Heather Christie for her influence in helping me to grow in knowledge and technical skills around Leadership and Personal Development. The skills have become critical drivers to my success in the coaching field.

Thank you, also, to all those friends who were kind enough to provide their personal testimonials for this book.

For the many discussions with my brother and sister who helped me come to clarity around our early family stories and lives together, I thank you both.

Finally, and most importantly, to my beautiful, wonderful, talented, accomplished, and—lucky for me—loving wife, Madge, for our fifty years of marriage and all of the life experiences those years bring including children, grand children and a great granddaughter. There is no better legacy— no better power—than family . . . and you will always be mine. It's the greatest power of all.

ABOUT THE AUTHORS

Iain Macfarlane is the President and Founder of **BizCOACHING & Associates, LLC**, that he founded in April 2004. Based in Madison, Wisconsin, the company is a franchise of **ActionCOACH Business Coaching** that is the World's Number One Business Services Franchise (*Entrepreneur Magazine*, Jan. 2012). **ActionCOACH** began in 1993 and currently has over 1,000 coaches in more than sixty-five countries worldwide.

In March 2006, Iain Macfarlane was awarded *Coach of the Year* **ActionCOACH North America** for 2005 and in 2009 through 2015 he was awarded *Best Client Retention, North America,* and in 2012 through 2016, *Best Client Retention, Global.* In 2007 he became a **Global Trainer** for new coaches of **ActionCOACH** and he also certified as an **Executive Coach** with *The Center for Executive Coaching*. In 2008, he certified as a **Strategic Planning & Operational Planning Consultant** to work with CEO's, Boards of Directors and executive management teams for mid to large companies. He has also received a number of global coaching awards including *ActionCLUB Award, Global*

for 2010 and 2015, *Best Executive Coaching Business Results, Global* for 2010 and in August 2012 he was inducted into the **ActionCOACH *Global HALL OF FAME.***

Iain spent his pre-school years growing up on a sheep and wheat station in the outback Western Australia before moving to Sydney where he completed his schooling through university. After receiving his Bachelor of Economics degree with Honors from the University of Sydney and certifying as an Associate of the Australian Society of Accountants, he received a Fellowship to attend graduate studies in the U.S. that included the East-West Center at the University of Hawaii, Columbia University and the Harvard Business School. Iain's early business career was in packaged goods marketing in the U.S. and then back in Australia. After successfully building the fastest growing advertising agency in Australia that he had formed with two creative partners in 1972, he moved to the U.S. with his family in 1978 after selling this company to Doyle Dane Bernbach (DDB), a leading international advertising agency headquartered in New York City.

Iain spent six years heading up Polaroid International and Atari advertising for DDB during the years of major growth for these two companies. During the next twenty years in the U.S., he held positions as President and CEO of five mid-size growth companies on behalf of venture capitalists and investment groups resulting in the eventual sale of these companies to generate the liquidity paths for the investors.

Iain has now taken this experience of successfully building businesses to form his own Business and Executive Coaching and Consulting company in 2004 with the objective to help other mid-size business owners, CEO's and corporate executives achieve their next level of growth and financial success for the businesses that is consistent with the goals of the business owner or corporate ownership. In 2009, Iain became the weekly host on Madison 1670 WTDY of *"The Iain Macfarlane Business Program"* to provide advice to business owners and business executives. Iain has been married for fifty years and has four children, five grandchildren and one great grandchild all living in the U.S. He is an avid sportsmen, photographer and enjoys worldwide travel. He also serves on two Boards of Directors.

Iain can be contacted by email at:
iainmacfarlane@actioncoach.com

Through his website at:
www.actioncoach.com/iainmacfarlane

Or on his electronic resource hub at:
www.rejilaberje.com/iain-macfarlane.html

Working with Iain to create this powerful story was **Reji Laberje**, Owner and Creative Director of Reji Laberje Writing and Publishing (RLWP), where they use meaningful writing to, for, and from you to make far-reaching, positive impacts. Reji's company stands behind bestsellers and storytellers, alike as they use their vision to work toward a better world through better words, whether those words are spoken, written, in book form, or created for websites and marketing documents.

Reji is a Bestselling Author whose books have been enjoyed by tens of thousands of readers. Her fortieth book hits the presses this year. As an Air Force veteran with a degree in international communications, she enjoys transcending genres, writing solo and with partners, including Dick Vitale, Bob Brenner, and other positivity endorsers, as well as alongside great illustrators through her children's books from respected industry leaders like Triumph Books, the number one sports publisher in the nation.

Constantly in awe of Iain, a man of great accomplishments and humility to whom she refers to as the "real-life Forrest Gump" due to how many lives and events he's touched, Reji felt truly blessed for the opportunity of working on *The Power of I Am...So I Can.*

Laberje, and her team of professional authors, editors, marketers, publishers, and presenters are available to co-write your life story or positive message and her company has a variety of content and publishing options available ranging from straight-to-publish packages for completed works, co-writing packages that match you with professional authors, and partnerships to help you create books under your own publishing label. All RLWP offerings include various levels of marketing and distribution, as well.

Reji lives and serves in her community near Milwaukee, Wisconsin, with her active home of seven people (and four pets).

Learn more at **www.rejilaberje.com**.

Iain and Reji stand exhausted after
a very full (and fulfilling) year and a half of work on
"The Power of I Am . . . So I Can"

"Love is the greatest legacy of all."

~I.M.

Printed in Great Britain
by Amazon